DO YOU BELIEVE . . .

- a good job or profession is the best way to make money?
- the best way to use a bank is to put your money in and leave it there?
- there is a limit to how much you can earn?
- desiring a great deal of money makes you greedy, unlovable?
- that bad news about the economy is bad news for you?
- that other people and the general economy are mainly responsible for your current money situation?

When you answer "no" to these questions, you are on the way to discovering the enriching truth about the road to prosperity. You are ready to have MONEYLOVE's practical exercises and techniques turn your positive thinking about money into a life of abundance, filled with love and creativity—and all the cash you want. You deserve it—and you can get it with

MONEYLOVE

MONEYLOVE

How to Get the Money You Deserve for Whatever You Want

by JERRY GILLIES

WARNER BOOKS

A Time Warner Company

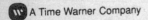

To Maggie Davis

ACKNOWLEDGMENTS

Leonard Orr laid the foundation for this book with his ideas, his famous Money Seminars, and his encouragement. It's often been said, but never more sincerely meant: This book wouldn't have been possible without him.

To my mother, Minnie Gillies, a debt of gratitude for all the healthy money habits she stimulated and inspired. These had a far deeper effect on me than the times she's wondered when I was going to settle down and get a steady job.

A hug of appreciation to one of the most prosperous people I know, Vicki Johnson, for her valuable assistance. Another hug to Dr. Moshe Davidowitz for organizing my Money-love seminars and coming up with so many prosperous ideas.

And to Julie Coopersmith, my agent and friend, warm thanks for believing in my prosperity almost as much as I have.

ADDITIONAL RESOURCES

Jerry Gillies

For information on his workshops, MONEY-LOVE tapes, and other books, or just to offer your comments and success stories, write:

JERRY GILLIES
MONEYLOVE SEMINARS
Box 1283
Mountainside, New Jersey 07092

Leonard Orr

For information on his workshops, money tapes, and publications, contact:

THETA SEMINARS
301 Lyon Street
San Francisco, California 94117

CONTENTS

Introduction   11

1. Do You Really Want to Be Rich?   25
2. Worklove   58
3. And the Money Goes Round and Round   111
4. Prosperity Banking   140
5. Prosperity Investing   164
6. Keeping Afloat Till Your Ship Comes In   182

Additional Resources   208

Introduction

You deserve to be rich, and you can be rich. MONEYLOVE can help you have a life of abundance, filled with love and creativity and, incidentally, all the cash you want. It's as simple as this: Thinking poor will keep you poor; thinking rich will make you rich. The MONEYLOVE concepts in this book will help you understand your money situation and what to do about it. Some of the ideas expressed here may shock you or frighten you, but they are all based on commonsense approaches to money. Here's a preliminary sampling of some of those ideas:

Spending money is better for your prosperity consciousness than banking it.

Money is an extension of your self-esteem.

You can't be emotionally healthy without healthy money attitudes.

You are probably, to some extent, living your parents' money script.

Financial satisfaction is better than financial security.

Enjoying your money will make it easier for you to accumulate wealth.

You don't have to work hard to earn a good living.

Loafing is one of the most creative, money-producing things you can do.

You can be as good a person rich as poor, probably better.

Worrying about money has nothing to do with how much money you have.

Money is something to be loved rather than feared.

There are a number of reasons I have linked the words *money* and *love* in creating this new concept. I know that will upset some people. Our society has often seemed to be divided between those who believe money is more important than love and those who believe love is more important than money. This book is an attempt to bridge that gap, and to say that money *is* love, love *is* money. Your money is an extension of your personality, and the more loving your personality, the more money you will attract and the more you'll enjoy that money. Statistics have shown time and again that those people who go into a business because they want to perform a service they love performing, or produce a product they love producing, make much more money than those who are in business just to make money. If you feel unlovable, chances are you will have a strong poverty consciousness. If you can't receive love, because you don't feel you deserve it, then you won't be able to receive money for the same reason. In order to be a really loving person, you have to be emotionally well, and you cannot be if your negative attitudes toward money are creating emotional problems. The strongest single factor in prosperity consciousness is self-esteem: believing you can do it, believing you deserve it, believing you will get it. Loving yourself. That love energy will go out to the world and come back in the form of money. One of my favorite examples of this occurs every day in a little restaurant I know. There's a waitress named Lil who is so filled with joy, so pleasant to the customers, so cheerful even after a long evening's work, that she just exudes loving warmth. And the customers respond. Lil makes a fortune in tips compared to the other waitresses. She's been there six years, and you'd think her colleagues would have caught on by now. But no, they go on their gloomy way in poverty consciousness, while Lil spends love and gets love and money in return. And she's not doing it for the money, she's doing it because she genuinely enjoys her work and the people she serves, and she loves the way they send love back to her. It's an indication of what the economy could be like if everybody practiced MONEYLOVE: not customers and servants, employers and employees, clients and professionals, but everyone sharing as co-lovers, sharing the process and the profit. This may seem idealistic to you, and of course it is, because not enough people

will overcome their inbred poverty consciousness to make it happen just yet. But if you
can't change society, you can change yourself,
and that's the most important transformation
of all. Pioneering psychologist William James
once gave three rules for changing one's life:

1. *Start immediately.*

This is why I suggest you plunge right
into the book, pick out one or two suggestions
that make sense to you, and start using them
now! Just for it to become clear that you *want*
to be prosperity-conscious can be the first step.

2. *Do it flamboyantly.*

The seven Prosperity Banking Accounts
in Chapter 4 are a good example of flamboyant
change, and there are lots more dramatic prosperity programmers throughout these pages.
Announce to your friends that you are now
prosperity-conscious, and on your way to financial satisfaction and financial independence.
If you make the announcement with love, and
they still resent you for it, you can offer to
share the information with them. That resentment would probably be an indication of
poverty consciousness, and you cannot change
other people until they are ready to do it
alone, so if they don't respond favorably, drop
it. People who can't handle your prosperity
consciousness aren't giving you the nourishment and support you need anyway, so you
will most likely be better off removing them
from your life.

3. *No exceptions.*

Exceptions are major obstacles to real change—going on a diet, for example, but saying, "I'll just forget my diet for today." Or starting a prosperity consciousness program for yourself and saying, "I'll act this way from now on, except in front of my parents." Exceptions are a way the negative parts of you weaken your resolve and dilute your active decisions.

There are many exercises in this book, and they will stimulate thought and facilitate change for you, *if you use them.*

I invite you to pick and choose your favorite techniques to raise your own prosperity consciousness. Some will appeal to you more than others. If any make you feel uncomfortable, chances are it's because your old poverty consciousness programming is at work resisting change. That old phrase by Samuel Taylor Coleridge, "That willing suspension of disbelief," can provide a useful tool. If you can suspend your disbelief that you deserve to enjoy your money, even for a moment, then you can actually start enjoying, despite any fears or anxieties. I find the most resistance to the MONEYLOVE concept from people who are trained to think analytically, particularly lawyers, engineers, and accountants. It is most difficult for these professionals, trained as they are in logical, rational thought, willingly to suspend their disbelief. I remember making a statement in one seminar that spending money can make you as prosperous as putting it in the bank. An accountant in the audience raised his hand and said, "But if you leave money in the bank long enough, with compounded interest, you will be substantially ahead." I responded, "That sounds like arithmetic to me, and I was talking about getting the most for your money in terms of pleasure and building an attitude that would enable you to creatively produce more money. Sacrificing the current use of your money, to put it in the bank, usually indicates a neurotic need for security, and the kind of fears that come from poverty consciousness." Now, I'm not saying you shouldn't have money in the bank. In fact, there's a whole chapter coming up on Prosperity Banking. But it's important to understand that the more current enjoyment you get from your money, the more predisposed you will be to create more wealth for yourself, and the more fulfillment you will receive when you do accumulate a great deal of money.

As long as you have a clear vision of what you want, and the inner determination to get it, the money will come. Money, after all, is just a vehicle to take you to your desires. As in driving to the seashore, if you are going to spend all your time worrying about the car breaking down, you'll miss the fun of the trip! And yet people do worry about money. For some, it is the overriding concern in their lives. Couples break up over money conflicts, people commit suicide over money, others become emotionally immobilized by neurotic expectations of losing their money, and still others rob, kill, and lie for money. And all of these attitudes or actions are manifestations of poverty consciousness. If you focus attention on the lack of money, that's what will get reinforced. Where you put your attention is what gets nourished. Poverty comes to the person who is emotionally and intellectually prepared for it. Wealth is attracted to the person who is emotionally and intellectually ready to accept it, expect it, and enjoy it. Poverty consciousness will overwhelm you if you don't have a personal program for prosperity.

So-called money problems are not problems at all but results that are dissatisfying. If you get results that don't satisfy you, it is because you are doing something to achieve those results. Many people want their money problems solved without changing what they are doing to achieve those results, and some even without becoming *aware* of what they are doing. This is magic. Prosperity consciousness is not magic, though, because it works so well, people often attribute magical powers to it. But it won't work at all if what you are doing to produce "money problems" is feeding your poverty consciousness with fears and negative reinforcement. You have to change what you are doing if you want to change the results, results which you may be calling a "problem."

Everyone in our culture has some degree of poverty consciousness. It would be impossible not to, considering all the negative money programming we receive from parents and the various media, such as books, television, and movies. If you can answer yes to any of the following questions, you'll have some inner resistance to prosperity consciousness. Count any response that isn't an immediate and strong "No!" as a "Yes."

1. Do you believe loafing and daydreaming must prevent you from being successful?
2. Do you believe spending money will make you poor, while saving it will make you rich?
3. Do you believe other people and the general economy are mainly responsible for your current money situation?
4. Do you believe a good job or profession is the best way to make lots of money?
5. Do you believe your parents' ability to enjoy the money they had was limited?
6. Have you made a strong effort to avoid frivolous spending?
7. Does negative news about the economy start you worrying about money?
8. Do you believe the best way to use a bank is to put your money in and leave it there?
9. Do you believe there is a limit to how much you can earn?
10. Do you believe you won't ever become financially independent?
11. Do you believe money is inherently evil?
12. Do you believe desiring a great deal of money makes you greedy or unlovable?

If you answered "No!" to all or to a majority of the questions, you probably are capable of becoming prosperity-conscious without much effort, and with hardly any difficulty.

Many of the techniques and methods described in this book are specifically designed to replace negative programming with positive programming. You'll find the personal Prosperity Proclamations particularly effective in this.

One of the most revolutionary ideas contained in MONEYLOVE is the premise that hard work won't make you rich or financially secure. Most people end up, after working forty hours a week, barely surviving on a retirement pension or Social Security payments, with less income to spend than when they were working. This isn't security, it's economic slavery, wherein you become a slave to the results of lifelong poverty consciousness. The only way to get ahead financially, and be able to enjoy it, is to come up with services and products and ideas worth money. By having a healthy attitude toward money, and using your creative mind to produce valuable ideas, you will thrive. The objective of MONEYLOVE is to help you get to a position where you are living easily and happily in your chosen environment, without money worries, and with an awareness of your own unlimited financial potential. And it doesn't matter how little or how much money you have to start with!

When I left a lucrative broadcasting career in New York in 1970, to start using my creative imagination to develop new techniques in meditation, awareness, and interpersonal communication, I was about $30,000 in debt. Using prosperity consciousness, I've now gotten to the point where, in 1977, I was paid $10,000 for a single idea that took me about an hour to create—and that was just a down payment, with a promise of much more to come! For several of those intervening years I was hardly solvent, with no regular income and quite a bit of debt. But I kept on, with the certain knowledge that I deserved to be prosperous, and that it would happen as long as I continued to do what I wanted to do. There were strong temptations in the form of job offers that would have gotten me back into the grind, and paid me huge salaries, but I easily resisted these. I was having too good a time to go back to work! Over those years I've talked to any number of men and women who were working at jobs they disliked, jobs that provided no pleasure or creative satisfaction. Many of these people cited as their fondest dream the desire eventually to have enough money to retire to Florida somewhere between the ages of fifty-five and sixty-five. I moved to Florida at the age of thirty-two! My life has been filled with all the leisure time I've desired, and organizations now have to pay me large sums of money to leave my delightful living environment, even for a one-day workshop. Though I do not yet have a million, I expect to get there by the time I'm forty. That's in two years! I don't need a million dollars to be happy. In fact, I doubt I could be any happier than I was when I was $30,000 in debt and allowed myself the freedom to do what I wanted to do. I am not desperately craving that million dollars; nor am I working day and night to get it. I'm not doing anything to get it—just expecting that, doing the work I love doing, I will be worth at least a million dollars in two years. And if it doesn't happen, it doesn't matter, because, in the meantime, I feel like a million dollars, and that feeling is generating more money each and every day.

The money that pours in when I have a valuable idea evokes a euphoric feeling. Not because of the money. The money is just a symbol of the energy and love people are sending my way because the idea works for them. I get the same good feeling when someone else makes a lot of money by using my MONEY-LOVE concepts. I actually got into the prosperity consciousness business by accident. For many years, friends have been amazed at my freedom from financial worry, even when I was heavily in debt and no income was coming in at all. I would tell them that wealth is an attitude and that I knew my ideas would pay off someday, that I trusted my own capabilities. These friends would ask me how I did it, and ask for tips on how to achieve this state of mind. The ideas I gave them worked. Conducting workshops and seminars in self-esteem and interpersonal relations, I realized that my money ideas were very similar to my ideas on how to become emotionally free and loving. In the past several years, there have been a number of systems developed to teach people new attitudes about money. I think these systems filled a need, since people were becoming more and more aware that their personal growth was often stifled by their money attitudes. The one man who seemed to be teaching the best prosperity consciousness methods was Leonard Orr. People whom I respected in the human potential movement raved about his workshops and tapes. I decided to investigate. I was amazed to find that Leonard and I had many of the same ideas about money, though he was more solvent than I. His money seminars helped me synthesize my own ideas into a workable format, and Leonard encouraged me to start presenting my own money workshops. When four people who attended my first prosperity consciousness seminar, at an event sponsored by the Association for Humanistic Psychology, called me the following week to tell me that the seminar had helped them change their attitudes toward money in dramatic ways, and actually helped them earn more money in just a few days, I knew MONEYLOVE was a concept whose time had come! The continuing feedback I've been receiving from people who have attended my seminars has given me tremendous support and nourishment in my efforts.

I expect to make a lot of money from this book. But making money is not my primary motivation, just a happy fringe benefit. One of the major premises of MONEYLOVE is that one of the best things you can do for your own prosperity consciousness is to lift someone else's. Every dollar you help someone else earn will come back to you multiplied, along with large helpings of love. A large number of people have paid me twenty-five dollars for a three-hour seminar, or one hundred dollars for an all-day workshop, and the information in this book is exactly the same information I've shared with them. In fact, I've elaborated and expanded each of the concepts, so that there is even more information in the book. I suppose a financial consultant would say I was foolish to put information in a book that I can get a lot more money for in seminars and workshops, and some of my moneywise friends have actually stated this. I emphatically disagree. This book is being written with a great amount of love and enthusiasm. I am excited about your reading these words and beginning to explore these ideas for yourself. I believe that achieving prosperity consciousness brings someone into strong emotional contact with everyone else in the world who feels prosperous and is convinced of his or her own personal worth. I welcome this connection with you, and invite you to share your success with me by letting me know the exciting things that happen to you as a result of living and learning MONEY-LOVE.

1
Do You Really Want to Be Rich?

Man was born to be rich or inevitably to grow rich through the use of his faculties.
   —RALPH WALDO EMERSON

The lack of money is the root of all evil.
   —GEORGE BERNARD SHAW

A feast is made for laughter, and wine maketh merry: but money answereth all things.
   —ECCLESIASTES 10:19

There is a powerful and persistent concept running through this book. It is not a new idea, and I did not invent it, but this entire volume is aimed at helping you accept and believe it. It is a basic truth, proven time and time again by people in all walks of life. I don't intend to hold it out as a tantalizing reward for reading my book. You deserve to hear it right now, at the beginning of your efforts toward a more prosperous life. It is the core of *prosperity consciousness* that, in order to be as wealthy as you want to be, you need just three things:

1. *A clear vision of what you want.*
2. *The belief that you will get it.*
3. *Practical skills to put that belief into action.*

THE REALITY OF MONEY

The basic reality about money is that it's unreal. Money is a myth. It has no value in and of itself. It is a medium of exchange for goods, services, and ideas. It's a beautiful human invention that most people haven't figured out how to use yet. Myths are wonderful things, made to be enjoyed, but if you try to embrace them, you'll just end up hugging air. So it is with money. For example, one of the most romanticized eras in recent history has been the Great Depression of the 1930s. People who struggled through that period love to recount tales of hardship, and warn that it can happen again. Now, I'm not saying the tales of pain and deprivation aren't true, just that they're not true *at this moment*, and they may never be true again. So living your life as if you were in the middle of the Great Depression is not seeing life clearly, is not seeing the reality of money.

I have a friend, a very talented therapist, who cannot seem to stop the treadmill she is on. No matter how much money she earns—and it's quite a bit—she never feels secure. No matter how high her reputation—and it's high indeed—she has the fear that her clients will stop coming, or not be able to afford to come. Her whole life is governed by her vivid memories of the 1930s, and she has said to me, "No one who ever lived through the depression can ever feel completely relaxed about money." I don't believe that and have seen it disproved hundreds of times. The depression had nothing to do with money. It was a massive collapse of the myth. It was a powerful display of *poverty consciousness*, in which people lost

27

their faith in themselves and the economy. Did anybody survive that era with *prosperity consciousness?* Of course. Though some of them don't like to talk about it, feeling those who suffered might be resentful, many people made a lot of money during that period. The economy had collapsed, but personal initiative was still present in isolated pockets throughout the impoverished land. The point is, the general state of the economy doesn't have to effect your personal financial situation.

YOU CAN BE RICH BEYOND YOUR WILDEST DREAMS

What is your reaction to that thought? Close your eyes and imagine a voice telling you over and over again, "You can be rich beyond your wildest dreams." Visualize the income and life-style you would like. Ask yourself if there is any reason why you shouldn't have them. Make sure you visualize what you really want, not what someone else wants for you. It's also important to keep your deepest specific aspirations to yourself; otherwise you will dilute your personal imagery and provide other people with an opportunity to tell you why your plans won't work, which many others will be only too happy to do. Do not get anxious or upset if your dreams don't materialize immediately. This isn't magic you're performing but simple, effective preparation for prosperity. And remember, those who have achieved great financial success describe their most exciting moments as the ones leading up to their attainment of wealth, rather than the actual moment of achievement.

Once you have a strong idea of what you'll do when you get the money, you can begin to focus on a specific amount that will allow you to do what you want. Don't just ask for enough to survive or to be comfortable. For six years I kept myself at a subsistence level by focusing only on survival. A major breakthrough in my prosperity consciousness was the moment when I realized I could ask for a surplus as well as mere survival. Instead of focusing on $200 coming in to pay the rent (and it usually did come in), I now focus on $20,000 coming in, so I can take a year off. I know it may be difficult to believe at this point, but that $20,000 came just as easily as the $200. As you begin to experiment with MONEYLOVE techniques, you'll find this will be true for you, too. People who say, "Well, I don't want much money, just enough to get by," really don't love themselves enough to feel they deserve more. They either fear money itself or fear that they'll have to do something unpleasant to get it. In addition to lack of self-esteem, these are some of the factors that cause people to avoid wealth.

It's a matter of asking yourself three questions:

1. Do I want to be rich?
2. Do I believe I deserve to be rich?
3. Do I believe I can be rich?

Remember the second item of the secret I call the core of prosperity consciousness: *The belief that you will get it.* This involves answering the three questions above with:

I WANT.
I DESERVE.
I CAN.

If you don't feel you deserve wealth, you won't enjoy life, no matter how much money you eventually have. Once you begin to feel deserving, you will feel desire. Most of the books and courses purporting to teach you how to make a lot of money list desire as the strongest factor. Some of them, however, paint this desire almost as an obsession. I suggest this is as destructive as believing you don't deserve prosperity. In fact, overwhelming desire may be an indication of poverty consciousness. Obsessive desire is hard work to build up at an emotional level. Prosperity consciousness is as easy as breathing. You may have already decided you want to be rich. In fact, that's probably why you bought this book. Once that becomes a clear vision, you won't have to work on it anymore.

Here's another little exercise in creative imagination. Make a list of ten reasons why you want to be rich. And then make a list of ten reasons why you deserve to be rich.

A DECISION

Once you decide you are going to be as wealthy as you want to be, you have made a commitment. Every decision is a commitment. I'm not talking about wishes, and I'm not talking about promises; I am talking about decisions, which are active moves you make in a certain direction. Decision is the beginning of action. At the very core of your consciousness is a decision residing: To be poor or to be rich. This is based on your past programming. It may sound simplistic to say it, but once you make a decision to be rich, you are well on your way to your first million. And *it is* simple. Not easy, but simple. It's not easy because of all the negative material you've absorbed through the years. This must be overcome before you can move forward. This mind-sweeping operation is crucial to developing prosperity consciousness. You may already have had an inkling of the possibilities, you may already be excited about your potential prosperity, and you may already believe you want to be rich, you deserve to be rich, and you can be rich. But that belief is not enough, until you accept it at a deep emotional level of consciousness. The reason most books on positive life changes haven't worked for most people who've read them is simply because they have overlooked the obstacles and not offered techniques to eliminate them. Until you identify and confront these emotional obstacles, you won't be emotionally free to achieve and enjoy the wealth you deserve.

THE OBSTACLES

Prosperity consciousness is a positive be-lief system. Poverty consciousness is a negative belief system. At each moment you can have only one primary belief, one primary feeling, one primary idea. When you have two beliefs, two feelings, two ideas, the subconscious will accept only the dominant one. And since your poverty consciousness has been with you a lot longer and gotten a firmer foothold than your prosperity consciousness, it will tend to dom-inate unless you put up a fight for control of your own mind! For poverty consciousness is always the result of what others have told you, while prosperity consciousness is the re-sult of what you tell yourself. You must remove as much of your negative programming as possible. You'll never remove it all. Wait, just wait a minute! Can this be true? Can an author of a book on self-development actually admit that you won't be able to become per-fect? Absolutely! I believe this book will help you get rid of most of your negative program-ming, but there's no way you will eliminate it all. You are a human being, not a machine. Part of the beauty of being human lies in being imperfect and therefore unique. From time to time, no matter how strong your pros-perity consciousness, a negative fear, doubt, or guilt will creep up from your subconscious. You will have the tools to deal with these little emotional gremlins, but accept the fact that you will never completely eliminate them. A further thought on perfection: People who try to be perfect are never original, never produce really creative and valuable ideas. In order to be perfect, you have to do it the way everybody has always done it before. Psychologists have long recognized the perfectionist complex as one of the most destructive to human growth and development. In terms of financial success, many people use perfection as an excuse. Making a statement such as "When I learn to do it perfectly, I'll start being successful" is a way to prevent getting started. Waiting for perfection in any aspect of your life will usually guarantee a deficiency, *a permanent deficiency*, in that area. Many people manifest their perfection complex by making "If only" excuses about their lack of prosperity:

If only I had more education . . .

If only the economy were better . . .

If only I could do it all over again . . .

If only I had chosen a more lucrative profession . . .

If only I had had better breaks . . .

If only I had been luckier . . .

If only I hadn't married so young . . .

If only my boss appreciated me . . .

If only my parents had money . . .

If only I could clear up my debts . . .

It isn't the man or woman who has it perfect who succeeds. People who have had all or most of the problems listed above have still made it. The attitude that seems to provide the surest path to success is one that says, "Sure, things aren't perfect, I'm not perfect, but I can do it!" People who make money often make mistakes, and even have major setbacks, but they believe they will eventually prosper, and they see every setback as a lesson to be applied in their move toward success. None of the select group of people Dr. Abraham Maslow termed Self-actualized was perfect. They suffered moments of guilt and sadness, moments of fear and self-doubt. These moments were few, and the Self-actualized people were able both to acknowledge and to accept that they were not perfect. Because of this capacity, they willingly took risks, were not afraid to make mistakes, and therefore were able to innovate, to do what had never been done before. The perfectionist is, at best, a superb copycat.

POVERTY CONSCIOUSNESS

So let's look at the attributes of poverty consciousness. People who are caught up in poverty consciousness:

1. Don't really know what they want.
2. Avoid responsibility for their own failure or success.
3. Always put things off.
4. Don't feel deserving.
5. Have limited curiosity.
6. Don't feel appreciated.

7. Are indifferent.
8. Are misers, hoarders, and prophets of gloom.
9. Rarely enjoy spending money on themselves.
10. Feel guilty when they don't have money, and guiltier when they do.

Most of all, however, poverty-conscious people have an unrealistic view of the power of money. They use money as a scapegoat, supporting the myth that they are unable to do a lot of the things they want to do because of lack of money. A number of my relatives were very upset when I moved to Florida, and a life of ease, at the age of thirty-two. They had been telling themselves that *they* would move to Florida, once they had enough money. As I'm writing this, six years later, they all have much more money than they did six years ago, and none of them has moved to Florida, though they're still talking about doing it *eventually!* That's a key word in poverty consciousness: *eventually.* Using it means you are not willing to do something now, or feel you cannot do it now, or are afraid to do it now. The difference between poverty and prosperity consciousness can be summed up in two quotes from famous, prosperous men. Jackie Gleason, in a TV interview with NBC's Tom Snyder, said, "I was poor, but I didn't know I was poor, and I always knew I'd make it." And the late Mike Todd said, "I've never been poor, only broke. Being poor is a frame of mind. Being broke is a temporary situation."

35

I CAN'T AFFORD IT

"I can't afford it" is one of the favorite comments of poverty-conscious people. It's often a lie, almost always an untruth. I was talking in early 1977 with Dr. Wayne Dyer, who wrote *Your Erroneous Zones* and almost single-handedly turned it into a multimillion-dollar best seller, by traveling around the country in his car and appearing on every radio and television show that would have him, even in the smallest towns. We were talking about efforts to promote my books, and he suggested I take off on a crosscountry promotion tour, just as he had. I said, "I really can't afford that right now." I'll never forget his response, coming directly from his prosperity consciousness. I taped that conversation, so I can share it with you word for word: "You've really got to stop thinking about what you can afford to do, because you can really afford to do anything that you decide you want to do." Largely as a result of that conversation with Wayne Dyer, I have spent much of 1978 traveling around the country, promoting my books. At the time, I related this story to a friend, who responded, "Wayne Dyer has a fortune now; why didn't he offer to give you financial support for your trip?" Because he believed in himself, Wayne Dyer was willing to believe in me. He knew I could do it. He made me aware of some of my own poverty consciousness and gave me the greatest gift any human can give another: He showed me it was possible and encouraged me to do it myself. No one's poverty consciousness was ever cured with a dose of money. If that were possible, the government's poverty programs would have been a lot more successful. The only way to cure poverty, which is a state of mind, is emotionally, and *each person has to cure his own*. All anyone else can do is offer support, encouragement, and positive examples.

Poverty consciousness is what we do to sabotage ourselves. There's a part of you we could call the "inner pauper" that will always come up with excuses, indecisions, and catastrophic expectations. The inner pauper is always motivated by fear—fear of failure, fear of success, fear of never making it, fear of losing it. Fear causes us to close our minds in tight little balls. Confidence allows us to open our minds wide, letting fresh ideas in. A woman friend of mine was very rich. She had earned it all herself in real estate. Rather than freeing her, this wealth tied her up in emotional knots. She was single, but wanted to find someone to share her life. Because she was afraid of being loved for her money, she refused to date any man who wasn't rich. She finally ended up with a millionaire, who kept trying to get her to turn over all her business interests to him! What she hadn't realized was that a man who had compulsively strived for a great deal of money was exactly the type to marry her for money instead of love. After her divorce she started dating a symphony violinist earning about $15,000 a year. I don't know how it's going to turn out, but she's certainly smiling a lot more now!

Whenever I run a seminar or workshop on MONEYLOVE, there are always one or two participants who are obviously being directed by their inner pauper. They sit smirking, as if to say, "This is ridiculous; changing attitudes about money won't get you money." These are the very people who will never use the MONEYLOVE tools and never even give themselves a chance to find out if they work. At the other end of the spectrum are those who sit with a calm look that says, "I believe I can use these tools and build my own prosperity, and I'm going to start right now." Inevitably, whenever I get a chance to follow up those who have attended my programs, these are the people who report tremendous success in achieving higher income and more pleasure in life. I find that when people say a workshop or book won't work, they are really saying they don't believe they can change. Just as when someone says he or she can't afford something within financial reach, this is a person who really doesn't believe he or she will ever be able to afford it. It's all part of a built-in self-destruction mechanism we all have to watch out for. Dr. Barton Knapp, a noted Philadelphia psychologist, says, "If you're going to do yourself in, your attitude toward money will serve as well as any other tool." Many people are committing what I call "temporary suicide" by shutting off potentially alive and enriching moments for fear of what it will cost, or feeling that they don't deserve to fully live and enjoy. The single most important financial freedom is knowing you can have a good and full life, whether you are rich or not. Prosperity is living easily and happily in the real world, whether you have money or not. Poverty consciousness can prevent you from living easily and happily, and you have to make an effort to eliminate it—wishing won't make it go away.

PARENTAL POVERTY MESSAGES

Most of the seeds that sprout into poverty consciousness come from parents. Dr. Daniel Malamud, a clinical psychologist in New York, has developed a concept called "seed sentences," which he says are messages from parents and significant others in our early lives, messages that have a potent effect on the way we see the world and ourselves in relationship to the world. Some seed sentences that may have led to an adult case of poverty consciousness are:

"When you grow up you'll learn the value of money!"

"Save your pennies for a rainy day."

"If you went through the depression *like we* did . . ."

"Don't spend your money foolishly!"

"Clean your plate, there are starving children in Europe!"

(This last one also led to a lot of cases of obesity!)

Can you think of the money messages your parents gave you? Sit down with a piece of paper and remember what they had to say about money and about your spending, earning, or saving it. Perhaps a little essay entitled "My parents told me money . . ."

What were your parents' attitudes toward money? If you had to pick two words to describe the basic money attitude of each of your parents, what would those four words be? And have you incorporated any of them into your current beliefs about money?

How would your parents feel about your becoming prosperous? Visualize telling them you've just become a millionaire. See their faces and their comments. Would they be happy for you? Or would they be worried because you now were more likely to be a robbery victim, or to have tax problems, or to spend it all foolishly? Parents are very good at creating "What abouts":

"What about security for your old age?"

"What about, God forbid, a serious medical problem?"

"What about protecting yourself against inflation?"

"What about the children's education?"

"What about us? We're not getting any younger, you know."

"What about your responsibilities and obligations?"

Any of these sound familiar?

Another way parents have of inspiring a negative view of money is by telling children they don't have time to play with them or have fun because they are too busy earning money to feed them. The implication here is that everyone would starve if someone weren't out with the proverbial nose to the grindstone. A parent's statement "I'm doing it all for you" is really a statement that says, "I'm doing it for my own neurotic reasons and using you as an excuse."

One of the great metaphoric phrases of all time has been appropriated by parents to conjure up an image of the difficulty in making money:

MONEY DOESN'T GROW ON TREES

What that has to do with any real-life situation escapes me now, as it did as a child. I *know* money doesn't grow on trees. I also knew that my parents, though of modest means, could afford ten cents for an ice-cream cone. It's as if you asked someone for love, and they said, "*You can't find love in an apple.*" It's a way of avoiding responsibility, of avoiding saying no.

What your parents actually did in terms of money also affects your emotional attitude. I will be forever grateful for two things my parents did that have dramatically affected the way I've lived my life. First, even if they had only $200 in the bank when vacation time

41

came in the summer, they would withdraw it and we'd go off to the seashore for a week or two. I remember my father's saying that vacations were important, and making disdainful comments about neighbors who spent their vacations fixing up the house instead of relaxing. The other thing was unusual for their lower-middle income level, and unique among all their friends and neighbors: Every week, no matter what the current financial situation, we ate at a restaurant on Saturday and Sunday nights. They weren't necessarily expensive restaurants, but in the postwar era of the late forties and early fifties going out to eat wasn't the national pastime it has since become. Those two habits, those two examples of prosperity consciousness, had a profound impact on me.

On the other hand, we had some relatives who had another money situation. The father of the family believed in keeping his financial affairs to himself. Even his wife didn't know how much he had in the bank. When he said, "We can't afford it," she had no way to be a part of that decision. I remember going to the movies with the kids and watching them unwrap their meager supply of coins, usually enough for admission only. I treated for popcorn and candy. My parents had always discussed the family finances openly and honestly. I knew what was coming in, and was consulted, even at the age of ten, about major purchases. I felt a part of the process. When my father passed away, I knew where all the papers were and exactly how much money there was in savings accounts and insurance. When the secretive father of that family of relatives died, the widow and children went through painful hassles trying to get everything sorted out. They hadn't even known whether he had written a will! I think a parent's keeping financial information so hidden and so separate from the mainstream of family sharing contributes to a poverty consciousness that stresses money as a thing apart from all other facets of life. Some parents have a lack of trust of each other and their children, with a fear-motivated feeling that they must keep a financial hold over the others in the family. Perhaps this includes distrust of the children, and a fear that they'll be considered more valuable dead than alive, particularly if details are shared about insurance and wills.

Another person I know has a mother who has a million-dollar business while her child struggles along in poverty consciousness, trying to keep the grandchild well fed and clothed. The mother pours all the money back into the business, saying, "It'll all be yours and your son's someday." Wouldn't it be delightful if that mother could feel prosperous enough to take out ten or twenty thousand dollars, which she could easily afford, and present it to her daughter and grandson as a gift of love. Even though I am well aware of the emotional fears and negative programming that lead to such actions on the part of parents, I still find it depressing that so many of them seem to prefer that their children should enjoy their money after they die rather than be able to share that joy while they're alive. Another sad factor is the passing of poverty consciousness from generation to generation.

I think it's important to state here that you can never change your parents' poverty consciousness. You can change only your own, and part of that change is being able to forgive your parents. They are doing the best they can. They may very well have been victims of their own parents' poverty consciousness. It's a well-known and tragic psychological fact that some people fail just to get even with their parents, as if to say, "See what a rotten job you did raising me!" Others avoid success to rob parents of the satisfaction of being proud. What many don't realize is that putting emotional energy into these negative efforts will produce only self-defeat. This is also true when you envy or hate people who have achieved success. Some people look at another's success as a form of punishment, as if that successful person were intentionally out-achieving them to show them up. Others enjoy and root for the success of another person, realizing it's an opportunity to learn by example, and proof that success is possible. Look within your own heart now, and decide whether you allow yourself to be put down or inspired by the financial success of other people.

If you are fortunate enough to have parents who are still alive, you may find them resisting your move toward prosperity. You're going to have to take some risks in order to make progress, and parents can always manage to come up with some good reason not to take risks. Understand that they may just be feeling insecure about your changing in any substantial way. And make no mistake about it, prosperity consciousness will change you! Reassure your parents if possible. If they are always complaining that you need more financial security, it's just because they don't love you enough to trust you and to believe that you are capable and talented enough to survive. You are probably much stronger than your parents ever suspected, and much more talented and capable. Eventually, when they are exposed to the joy you feel when you take your life and your fortune into your own hands, they'll begin to understand. Until then, just love them, forgive them, and don't expect anything from them. They already gave you the greatest gift of all: life itself. And with that gift came the most sophisticated money-making machine in all the universe: your brain.

AFFIRMATIONS

An affirmation is a declaration you make to yourself of something you believe or hope to believe. As the first step in substantially changing your money programming, you'll be working with affirmations, which I call PROS-PERITY PROCLAMATIONS. They will become a major tool in your battle against poverty consciousness. The repetition of positive and alive messages to your subconscious is the only foolproof way to reprogram your brain. Remember, when you have two ideas, the subconscious will accept the dominant one. Repetition is one way to make sure the good guys win, that the positive money thoughts replace the negative, self-defeating ones. You are using the power of suggestion, but, more important, you are getting into the habit of *positive action*. Positive thinking sounds great, and it's necessary for success, but you can positive-think from now until 2001 without changing your basic habits. It takes action to move forward, and thought that isn't followed by action is worthless when it comes to changing your life. The Prosperity Proclamations are the activating force. You can nod your head and agree with a lot of what I say throughout this book, but *until you start reprogramming your subconscious and thereby become committed and emotionally involved in your own prosperity, you will be doomed to failure!*

Realize that a part of you will resist any major change, that the part I call the inner pauper is frightened of change. Using affirmations, positive programming words fed directly into your computer-like brains, is an important breakthrough, a vital indication that you have made a positive decision to change your money attitudes.

Before going on with the subject of affirmations, and providing more guidelines for their use so you can start functioning at a new level of financial awareness immediately, let's pay attention to your reaction to this concept of affirmations. For instance, if I said to you, "Just repeat the phrase, 'I feel wonderful!' every day and you will begin to feel better," what would your reaction be to my comment? Would you feel I had gone off the deep end? Would you feel I'm promoting magic? Would you feel it couldn't possibly work? Or would you try it and see how it felt, and *then* decide whether it worked or not?

THE BIG SECRET

Let me tell you a fantastic, immense secret about human consciousness. I suppose it's the most powerful idea contained in this book, and one that countless men and women have used to change their lives. If you pay attention to it, it can help you change yours. The secret: *Your subconscious mind cannot distinguish between facts and imagined facts.* This means if you present imagined material strongly and vividly enough, it will be accepted as real! This is why your body responds with all the physiological attributes of danger —including increased respiration, muscle tension, adrenalin release, secretion of blood lactate which is related to stress, increased skin moisture, and rapid pulse—when you fear an imagined danger. This means that imagining you are wealthy and are producing lots of money will convince your brain, which will convince your body, and you will start to look, breath, walk, and act like a rich person! Sure, it's easier to feel rich if you're staring at a pile of thousand-dollar bills you're counting, but imagining those bills can be just as effective. All it takes is imagination and concentration.

I have been using personal affirmation in my workshops for the past seven years. I have never once seen them fail as a potent tool for change, once the person starts using them on a regular basis. People can come up with all sorts of reasons not to use them:

"It is beneath my dignity."

It escapes me how an affirmation can be any more beneath someone's dignity than living in financial turmoil, or talking about money troubles, or believing there is a limit to how much money he or she is entitled to.

"If it works, why doesn't everyone do it?"

Indeed! Well, it does work, and I suppose the reason everyone doesn't do it is because not everyone is ready for prosperity. You bought this book, or at least started reading it, so evidently you have decided you are ready to work on your money situation at an emotional level.

"I'd feel silly."

There's nothing sillier than not being wealthy on this rich planet with its growing economy. Doing something about it is the least silly thing any sensible person can do!

"But I want some practical suggestions!"

Thie is one of the most common objections. Some people come to one of my prosperity consciousness seminars expecting to be told how to balance their checkbook, or buy corporate bonds, or deal in commodities. The whole premise is, of course, that wealth is not material gain but a state of mind. It therefore can be easily achieved only by starting with the mind and its basic attitudes, *which can be changed if they are obstacles to prosperity!*

So much for the objections. As I write these words, I am excited for you, for I know how delighted and surprised you will be after using your Prosperity Proclamations! These are intentional beliefs you will start programming into your consciousness for the specific purpose of changing your negative attitudes about money. A lot of people attribute metaphysical powers to affirmations. I make no such claims, though I have seen amazing things accomplished in all areas of life with this method. I assert that these are positive signals you are sending your brain, so that it can begin moving in a direction that will provide you with all the money you want. If more than that happens for you, consider it a happy fringe benefit. Don't question it, just enjoy it. Again, we do not begin to know the total power of the mind. Repeated statements and sayings have done much to form the person you are right now, including the negative, nonproductive, noncreative parts of you. Using the Prosperity Proclamations is merely a way of reversing that process, in a highly accelerated way.

I am going to share seven Prosperity Proclamations with you. You may reword them if a variation feels better. You may eventually choose to replace them with your own, perhaps with more specific programming. There are several factors to consider when creating affirmations. First, they must be alive messages, not wishes. "I want more money" is a wish, not an affirmation. It must be a positive statement, personalized, to the point, easy to understand, and preferably one that will conjure up pictures in your mind. It must be action-oriented, with a feeling of movement, of aliveness.

THE PROSPERITY PROCLAMATIONS

1. A LOT MORE MONEY IS FLOWING INTO MY LIFE. I DESERVE IT AND WILL USE IT FOR MY GOOD AND THAT OF OTHERS.

One way of ensuring that this programming is received at a deep emotional level is to keep track of your emotional reactions to it. Repeat the sentences ten times to yourself. Stop and see whether you're absorbing it, whether it feels right at a gut level. Take a

50

deep breath, and see whether you can feel the proclamation click into your subconscious. If you have a negative reaction, don't repress it, bring it out into the open. Take a piece of paper and write out the first Prosperity Proclamation twenty times, leaving room for emotional comments. Then decide what your reactions are, and write them in, even if they are negative. For example:

A LOT MORE MONEY IS FLOWING INTO MY LIFE. I DESERVE IT AND WILL USE IT FOR MY GOOD AND THAT OF OTHERS.
  I don't know, what did I ever do to deserve this money?

A LOT MORE MONEY IS FLOWING INTO MY LIFE. I DESERVE IT AND WILL USE IT FOR MY GOOD AND THAT OF OTHERS.
  C'mon now, where's all this wonderful money coming from?

If you write your emotional response to each of the twenty repetitions, you'll find that your reaction will start to get more positive. You may want to write your response after writing each positive statement, rather than waiting until you write all seven proclamations.

The Prosperity Proclamations must be as believable as possible. Most of them are money messages that explain themselves. From now on, I will give some explanation of the particular choice of words. For instance, in the first proclamation—A LOT MORE MONEY IS FLOWING INTO MY LIFE. I DESERVE IT AND WILL USE IT FOR MY GOOD AND THAT OF OTHERS—the first sentence evokes an image of money moving toward you. This can be fun to visualize as you say or write the proclamation. Imagine the money coming to you in a river of bills. Part of believing you can become prosperous is believing that a lot more money *is* coming to you. I DESERVE IT is something you have to feel to accept it openly without guilt or apology, and WILL USE IT FOR MY GOOD AND THAT OF OTHERS takes a step further and allows you to conjure up images of how you'll use the money, giving yourself and others pleasure.

2. I HAVE AN UNLIMITED NUMBER OF VALUABLE IDEAS IN MY CONSCIOUSNESS.

This is absolutely true, and the sooner you believe it, the sooner you can start bringing those ideas up to the surface. I remember one woman in a workshop who complained she wasn't creative. Her husband supported this view, because he did some writing and liked to think of himself as the only creative person in the family. I had her make up a proclamation, just suggesting that it should be a sentence that, if she believed it, would change her attitude about her own creativity. She came up with I AM MORE

CREATIVE THAN I EVER BELIEVED POSSIBLE. At first she found this hard to believe, but she was persistent and kept it up. She had always wanted to work with her hands, so she tried macrame. She told me she didn't even feel the proclamation working, but one day she just sort of knew it was true! Her macrame work, in just four months, got good enough for her to sell at a local flea market. Then an interior designer saw her work and hired her to create original macrame pieces to blend in with his interiors. Within a year she was making a substantial income from her creativity. Even I was surprised at how fast it worked for her. But that's just one of many examples of the power of the mind. You might picture, with this affirmation, ideas crowding together in your subconscious, just bursting to get through to your conscious mind.

3. I LOVE WHAT I DO, AND THAT LOVE BRINGS ME ALL THE MONEY I WANT.

This is one of the core principles of MONEYLOVE, coming up in detail in the chapter entitled "Worklove." This could put you in touch with some dissatisfaction over what you do to earn a living, but repeating it, even under these circumstances, can have a potent effect on your life and your work. It's also valuable to understand that the loving energy you put into your work is what provides you with a large income.

4. EVERY DOLLAR I CIRCULATE EN-RICHES THE ECONOMY AND COMES BACK TO ME MULTIPLIED.

This Prosperity Proclamation is a power-house! It can change your entire attitude toward spending money. You'll understand it more clearly after reading Chapter 3, "And the Money Goes Round and Round." But it doesn't have to make complete sense for it to begin to work on your subconscious. Abstract thoughts are usually the most powerful, since they allow your own mind to interpret and adapt the idea to your individual needs. This proclamation also makes economic sense, since you do put any money you spend into the economy, and the richer that economy, the more money there is to buy your goods, services and ideas.

5. EVERY DOLLAR I BANK IS ACCUMU-LATED WEALTH FOR MY PERSONAL PLEASURE.

This one will make more sense after you read Chapter 4, "Prosperity Banking." Basically, it's a way to change your attitude about saving money, so that you have a more direct contact with your money in the bank. A lot of people are programmed to put money away for emergencies such as sudden illness. This associates money with pain in your subconscious and is a good way to keep yourself in poverty consciousness.

6. NO MATTER WHAT I DO, MY FINANCIAL WORTH INCREASES EVERY DAY.

This relates to two chapters, "Worklove" and "Prosperity Banking." In the first, it relates to the fact that, as a growing, creative person, you produce more valuable ideas each day and so become a more valuable person. In terms of banking, this is true because of interest building up in even a modest bank account. And all of this does happen no matter what you do.

7. ALL MY INVESTMENTS ARE PROFITABLE, EITHER IN MONEY OR VALUABLE EXPERIENCE.

This is related, naturally, to Chapter 5, "Prosperity Investing." Many successful investors have related to me tales of how they learned priceless lessons when they lost money on specific investments. In the long term, the sensible investor will gain. The short-term losses that can occur are merely guiding lights, pointing out the right direction. One of the investments I lost money on provided the spark that led to one of the valuable concepts I talk about in the investing chapter. But you go into each investment of time, money, or energy with the expectation that you will somehow come out ahead. This means also having an attitude of "If I don't get what I want, it's because something better is waiting for me." If you check out your personal history, you'll find that this has usually been true.

An easy way to absorb your seven Prosperity Proclamations is to tape them and play them back whenever possible. I suggest taping each one ten times. You might even choose to repeat them along with the tape. Modify them as you please, and even come up with your own when this feels right.

A couple of additional hints: When saying them, you might take a deep breath and feel your wealth increasing as you inhale, and all your negative programming leaving your consciousness as you exhale. This can be a valuable visualization for you throughout the day, with or without your proclamations. You might say to yourself, WITH EACH BREATH I AM INCREASING MY WEALTH AND ELIMINATING MY POVERTY CONSCIOUS-NESS. Another useful habit is to say silently to each person you meet, YOU DESERVE WEALTH AND THE FULFILLMENT OF YOUR FONDEST DREAMS. Time and time again I've seen it proved that the more you are willing to help others prosper, the more prosperous you will become yourself!

You have probably already had some emotional feelings that acted as Prosperity Proclamations. Have you ever set out to do something and said to yourself, "I can do this"? That's a way you had of convincing yourself, and it usually works! I remember one woman saying to me, "I always make money on the stock market." That, too, was a Prosperity Proclamation, and it became a self-fulfilling prophecy.

As you see the power of these positive statements, realize that the negative statements you've been saying to yourself and others have just as much power. Just this acknowledgment of their potential for harm will help you eliminate them from your life.

Saying "He doesn't deserve that job, I hope he doesn't get it" is a poverty proclamation of the highest order, and it will bounce back into your own subconscious. If for no other reason, avoid these statements to avoid damaging yourself.

You are the best-equipped person in all the world to program your own brain. Giving up this privilege to others is one of the most damaging things you can do to yourself. Using the Prosperity Proclamations will help you take charge of your own creative process. You might picture yourself in front of this sophisticated giant computer, programming in important information with confidence, with joy, and with the certainty that the information will result in positive action!

2
Worklove

*Consider the lilies of the field, how they grow;
they toil not, neither do they spin: and yet I
say unto you, That even Solomon in all his
glory was not arrayed like one of these.*
  —JESUS

*Greater even than the pious man is he who
eats that which is the fruit of his own toil;
for scripture declares him twice-blessed.*
  —THE TALMUD

*The crowning fortune of a man is to be born
to some pursuit which finds him employment
and happiness, whether it be to make baskets,
or broadswords, or canals, or statues, or songs.*
  —RALPH WALDO EMERSON

Work is love made visible.
  —KAHLIL GIBRAN

*What we call "creative work" ought not to be
called work at all, because it isn't. . . . I imagine
that Thomas Edison never did a day's work
in his last fifty years.*
  —STEPHEN LEACOCK

The richest man in all the world is the one who has a good time earning his daily bread. WORKLOVE means just that, loving the work you do, doing the work you love. When Dr. Abraham Maslow studied Self-actualized people, that tiny portion of the population who made the most of their human potential, he found that they all had some work they felt was worthwhile and important. They found work a pleasure, and there was little distinction between work and play. To be Self-actualized, someone must be not only doing work he or she considers important, but doing that work well, and *enjoying* the doing.

Psychologists far and wide have come to the conclusion that human beings can reach the heights of their true potential only when they operate as unified organisms. Having work separate from what is pleasurable creates disunity. Most people in the world today are working at jobs or careers that give them no pleasure, no excitement, no outlet for their creative imaginations. If most people are working at jobs they don't love, you can imagine what kind of emotional environment this creates, and how it would change if we all went to work with a smile on our lips and love in our heart!

As a human being, with countless valuable ideas waiting in your subconscious right now, you can be truly fulfilled only when you find a means of expression. This is a crying demand from your own consciousness, and to ignore it is to remain forever stifled, forever mediocre, forever dissatisfied.

Patanjali, the founder of Yoga in ancient India, as translated by Edmond Bordeaux Szekely in his book *Creative Work*, said: "When you are inspired by some great purpose, some extraordinary project, all your thoughts break their bonds: Your mind transcends limitations, your consciousness expands in every direction, and you find yourself in a new, great, and wonderful world. Dormant forces, faculties and talents become alive, and you discover yourself to be a greater person by far than you ever dreamed yourself to be."

You'll notice that so far in this chapter I haven't mentioned money. It's been intentional. Working at something just for the money is an act of poverty consciousness at its worst. It's saying to yourself, "I haven't the talent or imagination to earn money doing something I enjoy."

When I was working as a radio newsman and commentator, I always quit a job when it was no longer fun, when it no longer stimulated me. When I would apply for a new job, my interviewer was usually impressed with the fact that I left a job freely to find a more interesting and challenging one. And I always got a better job within a few days!

Many people give themselves a self-imposed prison sentence by working at something they don't enjoy, aiming for the day they can retire. Working to retire is poverty consciousness. It's saying, "I don't deserve to do what I really want to do until I put so many years of hard labor in." As I said, a prison sentence.

Deep in your subconscious, handed down from generation to generation, there are some ancient beliefs imbedded—beliefs that say work is a hardship, a punishment from the gods, something we have to endure while living this life. The belief is that it is natural to have to work hard to survive, that this is somehow dictated by the natural order of things. And with these beliefs so deeply ingrained at a subconscious level, most people find themselves in a frantic internal conflict, between what they want to do and the way they believe it has to be. Let's check out your own beliefs in this area. Answer these questions:

1. Do you believe a nose-to-the-grindstone attitude is the surest path to prosperity?
2. Do you believe it's frivolous to want to enjoy your work?

3. Do you believe work has to be a serious affair?
4. Do you believe your job determines how worthwhile you are?
5. Do you believe pensions and retirement benefits are one of the most important things to look for in a job?
6. Do you believe that you're supposed to work hard forty hours a week so you can enjoy your evenings, weekends, and vacations?
7. Do you really believe you deserve a job that is fun and exciting?
8. Do you believe going to work is just something you have to do?
9. If you left your current work, could you ever see yourself wanting to do it without pay, just for the fun of it?
10. Would you encourage a child of yours to enter the same field?

If you answered questions 1, 2, 3, 4, 5, 6, 8 "Yes," or questions 7, 9, 10 "No," you probably are the victim of those negative beliefs. In *Creative Work* Edmond Bordeaux Szekely wrote: "If you feel that work is a punishment or hardship, or if you have no desire for work, or live in the hope of retiring soon—do not think you are entertaining the thoughts of a wise man; you are merely dancing to mental tunes that savages played ten thousand years ago."

Patanjali taught that, with love and enthusiasm directed toward our work, what was once a chore and hardship now becomes a wonderful tool to develop, enrich, and nourish our lives. And this is the only kind of attitude to have in order to really prosper. A sense of accomplishment is what brings happiness, not the money you get for that accomplishment. In Karma Yoga, Patanjali taught that work should be the principal channel of expression for mind and soul. When your work is what you most enjoy, the love energy that this creates brings you untold wealth.

Stop punishing yourself! I suppose that's the message that will bring you the most money. You are a creative human being, not an ox. An ox can work all day just for its daily meal. Working at drudgery just to survive is something any dumb animal can do. Almost any noncreative task can now be performed by a machine. But you are still a creative human being, not a machine.

Ask yourself this: "Can what I do to earn a living be done by a sophisticated but unfeeling and unimaginative robot?"

Of course, the difference between work and play is attitude. If you are not enjoying what you are doing now, it doesn't mean it can't be enjoyable. Our deeply ingrained attitudes about work really conspire against our enjoying anything we choose as a way to earn money. A lot of people don't even enjoy their play. And exercise is something most people do because they think they have to do it. The nationally syndicated columnist Dr. Peter Steincrohn wrote a book some years back entitled *How to Keep Fit Without Exercise,* and he has angered jogging enthusiasts with such comments in his column as "I never see joggers smiling." But it's true that people seem to take their exercise as seriously as their work. It's a way to punish themselves for eating too much, or enjoying too much, or relaxing too much. And this, too, is poverty consciousness. Exercise that becomes hard work is a form of punishment. Unless what you do is done with love and joy, it cannot have the best possible results for you, physically or emotionally.

There's no way you will ever be able to buy back enough pleasure to make up for what you missed by not enjoying your work.

Jack is a young man I know who is determined to retire by the age of forty. He is working at a job he detests, and saving every cent. He even lives with his parents to save on rent. He'll probably make that retirement deadline, but I doubt it will be worth it. Whenever I talk to him, he asks me about all the fun I've been having in my work, and says, "Ahh, when I retire, that's how I'm going to live!" He'll have about a quarter of a million dollars by the time he's forty, but he will have thrown away twenty years of youth, twenty years in which he put all his energy into a job he hated. Jack is socially retarded. He just hasn't been out in the real world. It's going to be very difficult for him to stop sacrificing and start living. And there is no way he's going to be able to make up all that lost time! Jack may have a lot of money right now, but you wouldn't know it to talk to him. He gets no pleasure from his money. He gets no pleasure from his work. He gets no pleasure from life. And he firmly believes that's the way it's supposed to be! Jack is no better than an emotional cripple, and he may never recover.

The reason you were born was *not* to have to go out and earn a living. There has to be a higher purpose to life than that. You arrived on this planet against tremendous odds, and after millions of years of evolution. Life is your reward for surviving that struggle, for making it. Does it make sense to believe that you have to spend the rest of that life earning that reward all over again?

The well-known literary agent Paul Reynolds tells of a boat trip he took at the age of twenty-one. He met an elderly, distinguished-looking gentleman on the boat. The older man asked him what his aspirations in life were, and Paul responded, "To make as much money as possible." To this the elderly gentleman replied, "Oh, I can tell you how to make a lot of money." Paul said, "Tell me." And the man said, "All you have to do is find a town somewhere in America that is growing. There are plenty of them. Find a job in that town, any job. And immediately start investing 10 percent of your earnings in real estate in that town. In thirty or forty years, you'll be guaranteed a fortune!" Well, that sounded pretty simple, so Paul asked the man, "Did you do it?" And the man responded, "No. It wasn't worth it."

I love that story because it goes to the heart of WORKLOVE. What use is a lot of money if you've given up pleasure to attain it? What use is a fortune when you've forgotten how to laugh, to feel, to love? And make no mistake about it, a boring, frustrating, noncreative job will result in just those deficiencies!

Ask yourself another question: "If I knew that I would make enough money to be financially independent in twenty or thirty years, would I be willing to continue doing what I am now doing to earn a living?"

And let's look at that popular description of work: *earning a living*. Another poverty consciousness statement if I ever saw one. *Earn* a living? You already earned your right to life by being born in an abundant world. You are living right now, you don't have to earn it. How about saying instead, "I'm earning pleasure," or "I'm earning satisfaction."

Two of the primary goals of the prosperity-conscious person are financial satisfaction and financial independence. Financial satisfaction is enjoying the money you now have, and feeling comfortable and secure about your life. Financial independence is having enough money to do what you want to do without concern about having to earn any more. I prefer these categories to "financial security" because there is no such thing as security outside of your own consciousness. Even a multimillionaire can be wiped out, even a pension can fail to keep up with inflation, and there's been a lot of thoughtful opinion to the effect that the Social Security system will be bankrupt in our lifetimes. Knowing you have the creative imagination to always earn a living is the best kind of financial security you can have. Even worrying about security is a negative statement you are making to your own subconscious, saying, "Someday I won't be able to take care of myself, earn my own money, and I need money put aside for that time." When your subconscious hears a statement like that it starts preparing you for the slowdown you predict. Your subconscious is an obedient servant. I remember an old movie comedy in which a wealthy bachelor said to his oriental servant, "I'm fed up with women. I never want to see another one again." The servant threw out all his pictures of women and his address book, canceled all his dates, and wouldn't let a woman visitor in the door. Once you give instructions to an obedient servant, who may have no way of knowing how seriously you mean them, watch out!

VALUES

Values are those qualities you consider worthwhile and important. But a good many of your values are imposed upon you by society and parents and other important people in your life. Here again, the first humanistic psychologist, Dr. Abraham Maslow, made some important discoveries in his research into those superior people he called Self-actualized. *He found that their values are based on what is real for them, rather than what they've been told by the outside world.*

How about your values? Are they really yours? How important is money in your life? Did you create this idea of the importance of money? You probably didn't, and if you think about it, you can come up with the name of the person who first planted that idea in your head. Many people rush headlong into the pursuit of wealth, without ever considering whether this is a real value for them. I think the biggest crime against humanity is the steering of young people toward careers for money instead of for love. I also think the pitiful state of our medical and educational systems can be directly attributed to the fact that many young men and women got into medicine, not through any inborn desire to heal, but because it's a lucrative profession, while many got into teaching because they believed it was a secure profession. I know I wouldn't want to be operated on by a surgeon who's more worried about his fee than my health, and I wouldn't want to be taught by a teacher who's more concerned with job security than with how and what I'm being taught. When you are lucky enough to be served by the person who truly loves his or her chosen profession, what a difference! I have a good friend who was probably one of the most financially successful gynecologists in the nation. But he wasn't in it primarily for the money. He really believed in what he was doing. He believed in telling his women patients the truth about their health, and in teaching them preventive medicine skills. He had a strong sense of prosperity consciousness and put great value on his capabilities, so his fees were high. But no one ever complained, because he followed one of the basic prosperity consciousness rules: He gave them *more* than their money's worth.

VALUES CLARIFICATION

Values clarification is an entire science of human behavior. It's just what it says, a set of strategies to help you clarify your values and choose more appropriate ones if you so decide. Dr. Sidney Simon is the foremost teacher of Values Clarification in the world, in his regular position as Professor of Humanistic Education at the University of Massachusetts, and in his books, including the pioneer work *Values Clarification*, and his workshops conducted around the world. It was at one of these workshops that I was first introduced to what I consider an extremely effective way of looking at one's values in terms of work. Sid Simon used a chart to facilitate this awareness, and he has graciously given me permission to use it, before he's even published it, with the sole stipulation being that I don't change it in any way. This is a way of looking at what you hope to get out of your work. These are the rewards you hope to get from working, what you actually want from your job or career or profession. The idea is to rate each category in order of importance to you. First the chart, then some explanations.

WHAT I WANT FROM WORK

MONEY	STIMULATION/ EXCITEMENT	LOVE & AFFECTION	LEAVE A THUMBPRINT ON THE WORLD
Survival & Luxuries	Challenge	Colleagues	Change Individuals
To Give Others	Cutting edge of Newness	Boss or Bosses	Change Systems & Institutions
Freedom of Choice	Variety	Clients & Customers	Create Product with Long Shelf Life
Security & Protection	Be Part of Team Solving Real Problems	Family & Friends	Affect Family & Friends

USING THE VALUES CLARIFICATION CHART

The purpose of this chart is to help you discover exactly what you want from your work. You are rating these wants in order of importance from 1 to 4, with 1 being the highest rating and 4 the lowest. To start with, you'll be looking at how it is right now. What satisfactions are you looking for in the work you are doing now? First, rate the four major categories in order of importance. Each one gets a number from 1 to 4. You are thus asking yourself:

Am I working mainly for financial gain?

Am I working for the stimulation and excitement my work provides?

Am I working for love and affection?

Am I working to accomplish something important, to leave a thumbprint on the world as I know it?

Most of us have aspects of all four in what we do. Rate them for yourself.

Next, take the first category, Money, and rate, in order of importance:

SURVIVAL & LUXURIES (Food, shelter, stereos, and vacations.)

TO GIVE OTHERS (College for children, support family, donations.)

FREEDOM OF CHOICE (So you don't "have" to do what you don't want.)

SECURITY & PROTECTION (For your old age, medical emergencies, savings.)

The item you think is your strongest motivation for wanting money is ranked 1.

The next column is STIMULATION/EXCITEMENT. Many prosperity-conscious people cite this as one of their major motivations for work. Rate the categories:

CHALLENGE (Sid Simon describes this as enjoying getting in over your head with the feeling that you'll make it out.)

CUTTING EDGE OF NEWNESS (Being really alive gives a sense of newness to all work.)

VARIETY (Lots of different things to do, a many-faceted career.)

BE PART OF TEAM SOLVING REAL PROBLEMS (This can generate exciting group energy.)

Again, the four subheads for STIMULATION/EXCITEMENT are to be ranked in the order in which they are important to you in your current work. The next column, LOVE & AFFECTION, covers an area largely ignored by people talking about and exploring their reasons for choosing a certain profession. But it's a vital area. This one is ranked from 1 to 4 on the basis of who you are most trying to please in your work, other than yourself, of course. Do you most want the love and affection of:

COLLEAGUES (The people you work with.)

BOSS OR BOSSES (Where the money and promotions come from.)

CLIENTS AND CUSTOMERS (Would include students if you're a teacher, patients if you're a therapist or physician.)

FAMILY & FRIENDS (Are you working for the love you get when you get home?)

I really like Sid Simon's phrase for the next category: LEAVE A THUMBPRINT ON THE WORLD. It's the kind of creative imagination someone with true prosperity consciousness exhibits, and an apt description of the impact his Values Clarification work has had on education and psychology. Is this what you're working for: impact? And where is it most important for you to have that impact?

> CHANGE INDIVIDUALS (Teachers are often motivated most by this one, the heady knowledge that you've moved someone in a new direction.)
>
> CHANGE SYSTEMS & INSTITUTIONS (This is often the province of the idealist, and can be one of the most frustrating motivations.)
>
> CREATE PRODUCT WITH LONG SHELF LIFE (This can be any kind of a product from a book to a new medicine to a new way of doing something.)
>
> AFFECT FAMILY & FRIENDS (Of course, the occupation most strongly motivated by this one may be homemaker.)

If you look closely, you may find you are motivated a bit by each of these sixteen factors, plus the four main categories. To take this effective tool a step further, go through it again—MONEY; STIMULATION/EXCITEMENT; LOVE & AFFECTION; LEAVE A THUMBPRINT ON THE WORLD—with all the subheads ranked from 1 to 4, but this time the way you would like it to be, the way you want it when you achieve your fondest dreams. The first time was what you want from what you are doing now; this second run-through is for the work you would like to be doing a few years from now.

I have used this Sid Simon values chart time and again in reassessing my own desires and dreams related to my work. I am pleased to be able to share it with you, and deeply grateful to Sid for his generosity and his inspiration.

It was a revelation for me, and it may be for you, to discover so many reasons for working. I suppose most of us focus on money and enjoyment of the work itself as the primary motivations. And money is usually what people talk about when discussing someone else's job. "He's making fifty thousand dollars a year!" is much more prevalent than "She loves what she's doing and it sounds like a lot of fun." In fact, many people, especially parents, don't take your work seriously if you seem to be having a good time. Fun and work are a difficult combination for a lot of people to accept. "Silly" is the word used to describe someone who works primarily for pleasure, even if that person is also making a lot of money. And the judgments people make! I've been involved in the creation of a TV series, and the situation in Hollywood is a poverty consciousness addict's dream. There, if you're a writer earning $3,000 a week, you wouldn't be caught dead having lunch with a $1,000-a-week writer! Imagine being so caught up in a "money trip" that you ignore someone's creativity, personality, and aliveness, and focus on the size of his paycheck. Recently a vicious rumor was started aimed at assassinating the character of a well-known screenwriter. Word was passed around that he was getting only $30,000 for a script instead of his customary $100,000. He spent quite a bit of time tracking down the rumor, finally discovering it came from the producer his ex-wife was seeing and was an act of revenge on her part for what she considered to be an inadequate property settlement.

When money becomes the only way of measuring success in the world, a lot of resentment is built up when someone achieves sudden financial gain. Rather than ask if that person is enjoying the money, many people start to make hostile comments, such as "Some people have all the luck!" or "He must know somebody." Contrast this with the attitude of the people who live on the little island of Nauru in the Pacific. Because of their rich guano deposits, they are among the richest people on earth. They practice a unique ritual known as *bubutsi*. The moment someone strikes it rich, or has some stroke of good fortune, or celebrates a special accomplishment, any friend or relative can ask for and take his or her possessions. *Bubutsi* means "to ask for and take" and is a custom everyone seems to love, even the "victims." It is perhaps the height of sharing. If, for instance, you celebrated your twenty-fifth wedding anniversary on Nauru, your neighbors might come over and appropriate your car, and some relatives might make off with your furniture. And you would just laugh and enjoy their pleasure. How about that for prosperity consciousness?

LETTING GO

Letting go is one of the most difficult things to do. Like a trapeze artist, you must let go of the one trapeze bar before you can catch the new one. In many instances, that trapeze bar is represented by a stagnating, dead-end job. Understand this, however: Any job or career can be made interesting and profitable. So it's a matter of personal priorities. Do you want to investigate the possibilities in your current work? Or do you want to reach out in new directions? Remember, a decision is the beginning of action, not wishing or promising. Whichever you choose, you will be better off than if you don't choose at all.

Let's acknowledge here and now that letting go can be a scary business. When I left a lucrative career in broadcasting in 1970, I believed in myself, but I was also frightened. No matter how secure you are within yourself, no matter how much confidence you have, there's a part of you that will always respond to any change with fear, and sometimes just the contemplation of change will give you shaky knees. Pretending you aren't afraid isn't going to do you much good. Confront your fears, list them, get to know them, and *only then* will you be able to put them aside and move ahead. So write out a list:

THE IDEA OF MAKING A MAJOR CA-REER CHANGE MAKES ME FEEL_____

Fill in the blank with as many different answers as you can come up with. And realize how your body feels as you think about this. Often, by paying attention to the physiological changes caused by fear, discomfort, or anxiety, we can get rid of the restrictive effects of those emotions.

One woman who attended one of my seminars had this list:

THE IDEA OF MAKING A MAJOR CA-REER CHANGE MAKES ME FEEL:

That I'll make the wrong choice.
That I'll exhaust all my savings.
That I won't get a better job, or even as good a one.
That I won't be able to support my children.
That I won't have an outlet for my creativity.

Even if you are *not* dissatisfied in any way with your current work, it is useful to look at your emotional reaction to leaving it. You may be so emotionally attached to security that the mere thought of leaving produces anxiety. This could be called a "security addiction" in that you are feeling withdrawal pains as soon as the idea of giving up your security is suggested to your subconscious mind. This security addiction is a strong indication of some deep-rooted poverty consciousness. At one of my seminars, someone once asked me, "You sound like you expect everyone to give up their job and do what they want to do. If some communist government wanted to undermine our free society, wouldn't this be a good way for them to create the necessary chaos?"

The person who asked this question wasn't really being hostile; in fact, he was a lawyer putting to use his overdeveloped rational-logical conscious mind. I replied that prosperity consciousness could never happen in a communist country, where the government chooses to do all the reprogramming of its citizens, where you would *never* be free to leave a dissatisfying job and find something more appropriate, and where individual initiative is suppressed. In fact, I think the pervasive poverty consciousness in our Western culture right now does far more damage than any external plots could create. And I'm *not* suggesting you immediately go out and quit your job. Your current work, with an improvement in your money attitude, might provide you with all you need. My experience has been, however, that the best way to become prosperous is to use your creative imagination to produce valuable ideas, and the best environment for doing this is *not* working for someone else, is *not* keeping your nose to the grindstone forty hours a week, is *not* immersing yourself in drudgery day in and day out so you might eventually retire to a life of boredom and inaction. There is one thing for sure, however: No one ever stayed very long in a job or career if deep down he or she really believed he or she deserved better and was worth more. And prosperity consciousness is believing you are worth more than anyone else can pay you!

So, I hope you now have a much better idea of how you feel about your work. You may have decided that you can do better for yourself, and the next step is to find a direction.

A PROSPERITY CONSCIOUSNESS DIRECTION

The best place to go in terms of work is to that place in your subconscious mind that *knows* exactly what you want. This will provide you with a sense of direction. A fantasy trip inside your subconscious seems an appropriate method to tap into this inner knowledge. So close your eyes and get into as relaxed a position as possible, and imagine the following:

You are completely free to earn your income in any way you choose. Whatever you do choose will provide you all the money you want, so all you have to decide is how you would best like to spend your time. Once you decide what talents you most like to use, and how you would most rather spend your creative energy, you can start to make a list of the possibilities.

THE POSSIBILITIES

Each of us has more talents and capabilities than we realize, and we do ourselves a disservice when we place limitations on the possibilities. If you can think of a dozen things you can do for pleasure, you'll never be bored. If you can think of a dozen ways to earn money, you'll never be broke. And if you can think of a dozen reasons why you will succeed, you'll never be intimidated by temporary setbacks or by what other people tell you. Try it.

THE PLEASURE DOZEN

Think of twelve things that give you pleasure any time you experience them.

THE EARNING DOZEN

Think of twelve ways you can earn money.

THE SUCCESSFUL DOZEN

Think of twelve reasons you'll succeed.

See if you can't make a connection between some of the items in these three categories. In one of my workshops, a young woman who was working in a telephone company office put baking bread as one of her PLEASURE DOZEN. On her EARNING DOZEN list she put down the fact that she could always get a job managing an office, but she really didn't find this enjoyable or challenging. On her SUCCESSFUL DOZEN list, she put down the fact that she was willing to take a chance. The group members brainstormed with these three items and came up with several suggestions. The one the woman finally took a chance on was to organize a group of her friends, also bored with their jobs, into a homemade bread business. They rented some booths at various festivals and conventions, offering to deliver a loaf of homemade bread a week to any customer in town. In addition to the bread, they had a little booklet printed up that told the story of baking, and the significance of the term "daily bread," and why it was important for spiritual as well as physical nourishment that the bread one eats be baked with skill, love, the nutritious ingredients. When a major convenience store started carrying their bread, they were on their way to a fortune. At last count, eight women were earning their money from this imaginative venture!

If you want some help coming up with a connection between what you can do, what you like to do, and the reasons you believe you'll succeed, you might get a group of your friends together and have some fun helping each other find new moneymaking ideas.

A couple I know of wanted to meet the challenge of starting an unusual business, but they also wanted to live in a remote desert area. They listed, as one of their reasons for knowing they'd succeed, the "dream book" they kept, in which they pictured themselves becoming more and more successful. They decided to sell jet fuel, specializing in the growing executive jet traffic. They drew estimates and pictures of how they imagined the business growing, from a one-room tiny service building to luxurious hangars and a restaurant. They realized that they had to find a way to lure pilots away from established stopovers and get them to land in their remote desert location. They appealed to both the gambling instinct in pilots and their prime motivation for flying executive jets in the first place: speed. This couple offered to provide the fuel free to any plane they couldn't refuel and get in the air in ten minutes. Needless to say, their business boomed. A combination of dreams, clear thinking, and creative imagination produced a winner.

A recent survey of people who had earned fortunes at relatively young ages showed they all had one thing in common: the willingness to take a risk. If you would rather be broke than take a risk, if you would rather be safe than reach for that dangling trapeze bar, if you would rather return to the security of pre-birth in your mother's womb than savor and live life, with all its unpredictability, then you probably have a built-in defeat button that will continuously hamper your efforts to prosper.

ERRONEOUS ZONING HIS WAY TO A MILLION DOLLARS

Dr. Wayne Dyer took a big risk. He gave up a secure professorship, took all his money, loaded 400 copies of his book, *Your Erroneous Zones*, into the back of his car, and took off on a crosscountry promotion trip that got him on radio and TV shows in every state. It took a year of major effort, but he finally had a best seller. And he loved doing it! Wayne told me, "I think any book that has quality can be turned into a best seller, I really do. But I don't think you can rely on anybody else to do it, other than yourself. You have to invest yourself, your money, your time, your effort, your enthusiasm, and everything else into the book, in a totally unique way that nobody else has ever even contemplated before, and everybody else would say can't be done. I believe this is true not just for making a best seller. I believe it's true for everything in life. Anything you really want, you can attain, if you really go after it." Actually the title to this paragraph is a bit misleading, since Wayne Dyer will probably earn close to five million dollars from *Your Erroneous Zones*, and it took him only thirteen days to write it!

Here are some other questions you can ask yourself when looking for ways to break out of old earning patterns:

1. What did I get the most praise for doing in my life?
2. What do people often compliment me on?
3. What have people suggested I do more of?
4. What have I gotten paid for in my life?
5. What haven't I gotten paid for that I could put a price on?
6. What kind of job or career could most enhance and incorporate my growth and change?
7. How do I prevent myself from doing something new?

THE STIGMA OF SELLING

The last item in the above list has special meaning for me. I was working in a small radio station in Delaware at the age of nineteen. I was doing all kinds of things on the air: commercials, newscasts, record shows, interviews. The owners decided they couldn't afford to pay me my salary unless I was willing to go out and sell commercial time to sponsors. I refused to do this, thinking selling was beneath me; after all, I was a nineteen-year-old radio star! I sabotaged myself by this limitation. To this day, I don't know whether I would have enjoyed selling radio time, but I wasn't willing to try it. I might have picked up valuable hints on dealing with people. I might even have ended up owning a radio station, since many owners started out as radio salesmen. But I prevented myself from doing something new. Selling seems to have a stigma attached to it in our culture. Many people consider salespeople as some sort of lower caste. I used to feel funny about selling copies of my books at workshops and lectures, feeling I was somehow lowering myself—until I read something John F. Kennedy said to someone asking him advice on how to be a successful author, as the late President had been with *Profiles in Courage*. Kennedy replied that when friends or relatives ask you for free copies of the book, you should suggest instead that if they were really your friends and if they really cared for you, they'd go out and buy a copy. Again, Wayne Dyer came up with some positive advice by sharing his belief that, if you have something worthwhile to say or sell, you owe it to people to make it available to them.

Having a product you believe in, whether it's a piece of merchandise, a work of art, or yourself, is the first key to successful selling. If you believe in what you offer, your enthusiasm will convince people to buy it, rather than any strenuous effort to sell them. I'm not suggesting you become a salesperson, but merely that looking at your attitudes toward selling can give you some clues to your own poverty consciousness, and to some of the obstacles you may have put in your path. Do you feel:

1. That selling something isn't worthy of you?
2. Exchanging something you value for money is a less than noble career?

3. Selling isn't creative?
4. You wouldn't be able to talk someone into something?

Those are just a few of the common beliefs people have about the possibility of selling. I'm going to share with you a means by which you can earn an unlimited fortune and give your prosperity consciousness a powerful daily booster shot.

YOUR PRODUCT

Find something you really like, preferably something you own at least one of. If it's something others have admired, so much the better. Find out where you can buy it wholesale, and buy just a few. Carry one around with you until you sell it. Don't pressure anyone, just allow their natural curiosity about why you're carrying it around with you to surface. They'll sell themselves. If you feel uncomfortable asking for money, let them ask if they can buy it and let them make an offer. The important thing is to pick a product you are enthusiastic about and can sell feeling you're giving something valuable in return for a customer's money. Make a list of ten things you own that it would be possible to sell. Look around your home. Even if you start by selling something for three dollars that you make only one dollar on, this will start to program you for success. Even if you want a career that has nothing to do with selling, try this, as there's *no* career in which you won't have to sell yourself to others, and *to yourself*, especially during temporary setbacks.

Once I got myself into the habit of doing this, I found all sorts of things I would feel comfortable selling, most of all, however, books. I love books, and I found myself over the years recommending many books to people with enthusiasm. Why not, I asked myself, offer these books for sale? These are books I believe in and love, and I could even offer a slight discount. I purposely picked books that were unavailable at bookstores, as I didn't want to compete with the merchants who had so kindly sold the books I'd written. There are forty thousand books published every year, many of great value, and few that ever make it in the deluged bookstores. You might find a book in a field you're interested in and inquire about buying the rights to it and selling it.

We've gotten away from the personal touch, and you could help bring it back by selling something you personally value on a one-to-one basis. With the advent of major corporations taking over individual stores, much of the warmth in merchandising has been lost. When I was a high school senior, I was elected president of the Future Merchants of Philadelphia. I thought a career in retailing might be exciting. But when top retail executives described their reasons for entering this field, and little mention was made of the pleasure of human interaction, I decided to get into a field where I could communicate more directly with people.

You might start out with some small item that sells for a dollar or two and, as you are successful, build up to more expensive products. As you orient your subconscious to success in this personal selling project, you'll find more and more success happening in your life. Just as, once you learn a new word, it seems to appear all over the place, once you accept the idea, backed up by direct evidence, that you can be financially successful, it will begin to happen at such a rapid rate your head will swim! But if you don't give yourself success experiences, if you don't truly believe you deserve to get money in return for what you have to offer, then all the valuable ideas you now have buried in your subconscious will stay there, not feeling it's worth the trip to your conscious mind.

HOW TO MAKE A MILLION DOLLARS

Making a million dollars is the simplest thing in the world, once you expand this idea of one-to-one selling. Just find a product that sells for $2,000 and that you can buy at a cost of $1,000, and sell a thousand of them! That's it. You'll earn a million dollars. Think about it for a few moments. Can you come up with something of value that might be attractively merchandised and sold for $2,000? And once you sell that first one, your subconscious mind will get behind you and make it so much easier to sell the other 999. This is because you have proven at an emotional level of awareness that you are capable of making a lot of money. You have plateaus of belief in yourself. Each degree of accomplishment can raise your aspirations and your belief in the possible dream. And that belief frees a lot of your creative imagination, as you start to think of yourself as a person who is prosperous. We've all had moments of this potent belief, days when we knew everything would go well, and it did. Can you remember a particular instance when you felt, at a deep level of your consciousness, that you were going to come out ahead? See if you can vividly relive that episode in your life, and remember how it felt, how it looked, how you acted, what you said, and how it all turned out.

YOUR PERSONAL CONNECTION TO OTHERS

Selling something on a one-to-one basis also puts you in clear touch with your personal connection to other people. The dehumanization of financial interactions has done much to foster poverty consciousness in our so-called civilized world. It all started out with people having skills and trading those skills for other skills or products among their friends and neighbors. Then the idea of hoarding and creating a demand took hold, and this meant that people were more concerned with getting theirs than with sharing. This also meant that the more aggressive types took charge of money, and the gentler souls began seeing themselves as perpetually poor. Just because it evolved this way doesn't mean it has to be this way now! Just because a lot of money is handled in cold, impersonal ways doesn't mean it has to continue that way. It's vital that you understand the human factor in money. Using it as a direct exchange between you and another person for goods or services will establish a friendlier relationship between money and you. There are too many middlemen in our lives. On a more spiritual level, you'll feel the oneness of the universe. There's a big difference between working at a job you don't like and taking your salary and buying food from the supermarket, where the farmer has his product sold for much more than he ever got for it, and dealing directly with that farmer. Or, as a friend of mine does, raising your own organic eggs and hand-carrying them to your customers. We don't have to drop out and live on a farm to experience some of this human quality in our lives, in our financial transactions. There's also a sort of spiritual connection between everyone who is prosperous. A brotherhood/sisterhood, if you will, of optimism and confidence. And it is contagious!

SHARING

When you're looking for new ideas in careers, or in products to sell, ask the people who know. If you sincerely ask others for advice, they'll usually be willing to share the

information with you. The more prosperous
they are, the more willing they'll be. For the
more someone is willing to help others prosper,
the more prosperous he or she will become.
Every time I've shared a valuable idea, it's
come back to me a hundredfold. During my
early days in broadcasting, I was more fortunate than many of my colleagues and became
quite successful at a very young age. I always
went out of my way to answer questions and
offer advice to those men and women who
wanted to find out how to get into radio or
television, or those who wanted to advance
faster than they were advancing. I always
waited to be asked, however, since I have a
certain bias against unasked-for advice-givers.
(Though maybe all of us self-help book
authors fit into just that category!) Anyway,
some of those young men and women I helped
get into broadcasting, or get ahead, are now
top management people or nationally known
performers. I've never asked for anything in
return, but it's a nice feeling to know I would
probably never have any trouble returning to
that field if I so desired, and that I'd have
friends and supporters in positions where they
could advise or assist me. (I have no plans to
return to broadcasting, but my friends in the
industry do come in very handy when I go out
promoting a book on talk shows across the
country.) Be willing to share your ideas freely,
without hoarding them, without petty posses-
siveness. A beautiful reporter for the *Miami
Herald*, Beth Dunlop, has interviewed me

several times. I always give a lot of what I consider valuable information in those interviews, rather than just trying to talk people into spending money for my books or workshops. Wayne Dyer also did this on all his talk show appearances. Rather than selling his book, he shared his ideas, and this willingness to share sold the book for him. Beth Dunlop's articles, chockfull of information, always had fantastic results in terms of response. When I did a MONEYLOVE seminar and an article appeared on some of the concepts you've been reading in this book, dozens of people signed up for the twenty-five-dollar seminar as a result of the free information I was willing to share in the interview. And you make room for new ideas to emerge from your subconscious whenever you give one away!

FAILURE VERSUS NOT SUCCEEDING YET

One of the fears that keeps people locked into old patterns and nonproductive careers is the fear of failure. One of the narrow perspectives that fosters this fear is the belief that life is composed of either success or failure. This either/or attitude is a manifestation of poverty consciousness, since it prevents a lot of healthy experimentation. Trial and error is still the best way to learn something. When, for instance, learning to play tennis, you hit the ball into the net instead of over it, your body automatically starts to compensate, your brain sends signals to the dozens of muscles involved, and changes are made to do better next time. If you hit the ball beautifully over the net the first time, you might win some points, but you wouldn't develop your skills as well. In fact, I had a colleague in broadcasting who could have been a tennis champion, except that he was such a natural player that he did well right from the beginning, and he never developed the strong foundation of playing skills needed to take him beyond the finals in a tennis tournament. You learn anything by making an effort and recording the success or failure of that effort, and changing the effort accordingly. If you have failed in terms of money, and have paid attention to what you were doing, you've been developing skills that will serve you well on your quest for prosperity. And if you've never been broke, being prosperous won't taste quite as sweet! So while failure and temporary setback is nothing to seek and worship or embrace, it is a very human happening, and a part of most of our lives at one time or another. Looking at it as just a pause on your road to success, rather than a repudiation of all your efforts, is the healthy view.

FAILURE FANTASY

A very effective way to deal with your fears of failure is to confront them. When you are hesitating about taking a risk, or trying something new, just ask yourself:

WHAT IS THE WORST POSSIBLE THING THAT COULD HAPPEN?

And really visualize it. If you are thinking about leaving a job that doesn't nourish you, picture leaving it and not being able to find another one. Can you see yourself broke, with no money for food or shelter? Paint your fantasy as black as possible. Unspecific fears are the most destructive. As soon as you have a clear view of what you fear, the fear itself usually diminishes. We mostly fear that which we haven't experienced, and your marvelous brain has the capacity to experience through imagination. If you turn your abstract fears into specific fantasy images, you will have imagined the worst. This has a number of advantages. First of all, the reality, when you do take a risk, is never as bad as the fear. Also, you will have diluted much of the potency of a negative outcome by vicariously experiencing it. Some of the people who've attended my workshops and gone through a visualization of the worst possible outcome came back and reported that they weren't really as worried after having the fantasy. One woman who took a risk, and didn't have it work out as well as it could, said, "It was so much less terrible than what I imagined, it was almost a pleasure!"

Another way to fantasize away some of the negative aspects of fear is to imagine the worst happening as a result of your taking a risk, and then think of yourself sometime in the future, after that failure, now rich and successful, telling an audience about that failure, and how you learned from it and survived it to reach new heights of prosperity. You can even use this little fantasy if you actually *do* have a setback, to give you a more productive perspective. Sometimes we get so caught up in temporary passing events in our life that we lose sight of the total life process and the cyclical nature of things. If you could look at a chart of your life, you'd probably find that periods of temporary defeat were almost always accompanied or immediately followed by dramatic change and new forward momentum. Think about this for a few minutes, and see if it isn't true for you.

In fact, make a list of the TEN MOST DIFFICULT PERIODS OF MY LIFE, and check out how many of them signaled major changes in your life, changes that led to new and better things for you. I remember, for instance, losing my first job in radio. I would have probably stayed in that comfortable, sleepy little town for years if I hadn't been forcefully jarred out of my complacency. I was sad at leaving my friends, but when I got a job paying twice as much, and with four times the opportunity, I realized I was being given a chance to use more of my potential.

Self-actualized men and women usually had a number of early failures before achieving their major successes. Their willingness to risk failure was one of the things they all had in common. Frank Goble's book *The Third*

Force is about the psychology of Abraham Maslow, and focuses a lot of attention on Self-actualization. Goble writes of these remarkable people: "Because of their courage, their lack of fear, they are willing to make silly mistakes. The truly creative person is one who can think 'crazy'; such a person knows full well that many of his great ideas will prove to be worthless. The creative person is flexible —he is able to change as the situation changes, to break habits, to face indecision and changes in conditions without undue stress. He is not threatened by the unexpected as rigid, inflexible people are."

Some people would rather anticipate catastrophe than deal with the unexpected. But life twists and turns in many ways, and flexibility is one of the most important traits associated with prosperity consciousness. It sometimes almost seems as if some people are looking for obstacles to stop their progress. Leonard Orr feels a lot of poverty-conscious people are victims of deep hostility and are determined to "get even" with the world. They avoid winning because, if they won, they wouldn't have an excuse to get even.

Poverty-conscious people are wonderful at turning victories into defeats. One man I know was putting his house up for sale, as his son was getting married and he had been widowed for several years. He was frantically worried that he wouldn't be able to sell it, or would have to drastically lower the price. Instead he sold it almost immediately at the price he asked for. Now he began to wonder whether he shouldn't have asked for more, and worry about where he was going to live, since he wouldn't have as much time as he had anticipated to hunt for an apartment. He found an apartment he liked right away, and signed a lease. Now he began to worry about whether the new owners of his house would make settlement soon enough so he wouldn't be paying both the rent and the mortgage payment. They made settlement on the house almost to the day his new lease started, so now he turned his attention to worrying about whether he was getting all the tax benefits he was entitled to. His friends thought that once he had a large chunk of money from the house, he'd be able to travel and enjoy himself more instead of always complaining about money. So he now took all his money and put it in long-term bank certificates, and continued to struggle along on his modest pension. This story doesn't have a happy ending. The worrying man finally suffered a fatal heart attack. A prosperity-conscious person would have been overjoyed at some of the events of those last few years of his life, but he saw them only as bad times, anxious times, unprofitable times.

To a much lesser extent, a friend of mine also created some negative experiences from a positive happening. She was offered a chance to do some consultation work for a government agency. First she worried that her boss wouldn't give her the time off. When she got that, she worried that the government agency wouldn't pay her an amount equal to her salary, which was about $300 a week. When the government agency gave her an indication that she would earn about $150 a day, she was overjoyed. But then when it got down to specifics, it looked as if she'd get only $100 a day. She had begun to count on that $750 and was bitterly disappointed. Here she was getting at least $200 more than her regular salary, and she was disappointed. She felt terrible about this for the four weeks before the assignment, which was to last a week. When it was all over, because of some new bureaucratic technicalities she got $800 for the week. Did she jump up and down for joy? Guess again. She was enraged that the government had put her through so many changes and "created" so much tension and worry. Of course, it wasn't anyone but herself creating all that worry and tension!

LAW OF INCREASE

An important realization for you is something many people have called the LAW OF INCREASE, which states that things will always get better, you will always ride an upward earnings pattern, real estate values will always go up, good stocks will always be higher five years from now than they are today. Generally speaking, all these things are true. Specifically, this is true for you, in terms of the value of your ideas. If you have a good idea today, and believe in yourself, chances are you will have a better one tomorrow. Most of us tend to increase our incomes from year to year. Look back on your life, and check whether it's true that things have always gotten a bit better as life moved on. This sense of upward momentum, the LAW OF INCREASE, is part of the basic prosperity cycle we are all a part of. If you recognize it, and allow it to become a part of your awareness, you'll know that things are always going to get better, sometimes even in spite of all your fears and worries.

The LAW OF INCREASE can also help you understand that there's no rush. There's no opportunity that won't be there tomorrow, and chances are an even better one will present itself. It's not healthy to procrastinate, or tie yourself up in knots of indecision, but neither is it healthy to rush into things without checking out your deepest feelings about them, without giving your creative mind a chance to choose freely. People rushing about after a "fast buck" are usually mired in poverty consciousness. I have often found that someone who is trying to urge me to rush into some business deal is really having his own doubts about the worthiness of the project, but wants to justify all the money he invested, so he convinces himself it will all work out in the process of trying to convince me! I've known a lot of people who have missed opportunities because of fear, because of feeling undeserving, because of lack of perception, because of the unwillingness to take a risk, but I've never known anyone to miss a real opportunity by taking the time out to assess its value carefully, and calmly move ahead.

SUCCESS MUCH STRONGER

Success is the natural course of events. It's a much stronger concept than failure, because it's backed up by real experience rather than a lot of negative fantasy. It is also easier to be successful. *It takes a lot more energy to fail than to succeed, since it takes a lot of concentrated energy to hold on to beliefs that don't work.* Try a little experiment. Take about five minutes and tell an imaginary listener about all the times you've failed, all the disappointments, all the frustrations. Then take another five minutes and talk about all your successes, all the times you've been praised and appreciated, all the good ideas you've had, all the people who've gone out of their way to be your friends, all the accomplishments. Tune into yourself and see which experience was the most tiring, the most debilitating. I'd be willing to bet the success monologue, once you got going, felt a lot better. That good feeling can generate fantastic amounts of energy. Failures are almost always individual events, while success breeds success and creates its own momentum.

CREATIVE LAZINESS

This has been one of my most controversial concepts, since most people are taught that laziness is an evil trait that inhibits growth, negates progress, and is death to ambition. On the contrary, I've found that a healthy regard for laziness can stimulate growth, can allow you to take quantum leaps forward, and is a sign of true ambition, rather than a frenzied rush forward into limited values and rigid goals. Self-reflection, for example, is one of the most productive things you can do with your creative imagination. Most of us dream of a day when we can lean back and relax. But that day is here now. You don't have to be a millionaire to take a day off and loaf. It's poverty consciousness to imagine that you can't do that right now. It's saying, "If I slow down for an instant, it will all go down the drain."

When I was director of the Biofeedback Institute, I trained a number of top executives in major corporations in relaxation and meditation. And I demonstrated to them that by slowing down, they'd be able to tap into deeper levels of their subconscious and come up with more valuable ideas. One publishing executive I trained started taking Wednesdays off to relax and meditate. He reported back to me that he got much more work accomplished in the remaining four days than he had ever gotten done in five! I've experienced this in my own life. I usually have a year-long deadline on a book. Many writers take at least that long to finish an average-length work of nonfiction. I usually take it easy for eleven months and surge into high gear the last month of my deadline. And I find it easier to write that book in a month than many others do in a year!

Sometimes I do get caught up in work, plunging ahead at a feverish pace. At times like these, I force myself to take a day off and do absolutely nothing, as an act of mental/emotional discipline. And the work always gets done, often ahead of schedule. The poverty-conscious fear that keeps us from slowing down is perhaps the most insidious barrier of all to prosperity. Most major achievers in this world have reported that they made some powerful breakthroughs after taking time out for contemplation and reassessment. Pay attention to what your belief system may be telling you right now about these last three paragraphs. Your inner pauper may be fighting the concept of Creative Laziness, and the idea that forced loafing is better than forced labor, and the thought that, by taking time out for regeneration and relaxation, you'll produce even more of value and worth. Even if you don't see immediate results, you'll be getting a powerful mental image of yourself as someone who can afford to take it easy. As James Thurber once wrote: "It is better to have loafed and lost than never to have loafed at all."

IDLENESS IS A MYTH

Of course, idleness doesn't really exist. You may be loafing, but you're not idle. Your brain is still performing its millions of chores, your creative imagination is still going ahead full blast, and your body is still going through all of its changes. Laziness is truly the mother of creativity. If your body and conscious mind are idle, your subconscious mind, your creative mind, can plunge full steam ahead, and your conscious mind will have room for those new ideas to pop up. A busy life will keep you from tapping into a lot of your potential creativity. Many people feel they have to prove something by always appearing busy. Part of the negative legacy of the puritan work ethic is this "busyness business." And have you ever noticed how similar those two words are? The creative mind is a split-second operation. This has been proved by people forced to cut their schedule because of health, who have then found they produced as much as ever. Here's a MONEYLOVE LAW OF WEALTH you can really have fun with:

A TASK WILL ALWAYS EXPAND TO FILL THE AMOUNT OF HOURS YOU DEVOTE TO IT.

A businessman I know gave himself three years to turn a profit, firmly believing that working very hard for that amount of time would produce results. And it did! But another businessman, in a very similar field, went into his business with the attitude that he had something very valuable to sell, that people would rush to buy his service, and that he would begin making money immediately. And this is what happened for him! Check out in your own experience whether you don't fill time with busy work, when you could actually produce your achievements in much less time. You have to love and trust yourself enough to let go. If you feel you deserve to be rich, you must feel you deserve to have more leisure time. *Now* is your only reality, and the leisure time you take now is the only leisure time that will prepare you for the future. It provides an incentive to earn more of it, and a time to form those all-important clear visions of what you want. Here are some ways to give yourself these Creative Laziness experiences:

AN UNEXPECTED DAY OFF

Just take a day off and loaf it away to your heart's content. Even if you have to say you're sick, get away from your routine. Pick a day you would never normally be off. See what it feels like to be a member of the leisure class for an entire day.

THE BETWEEN-JOBS VACATION

We all change jobs from time to time. The tendency often is to rush right into the new job. Give yourself a treat. Imagine it took you an extra month to find this new job, and enjoy that month as a reward for getting the new job. Inner doubt is the only thing that prevents us from asking for a delay in the starting date of employment. If you are valuable today, you'll be even more valuable a month from now. And it isn't bad psychology to let your new boss know you feel prosperous enough to take a whole month off without pay!

THE CONTEMPLATION-OF-ASSETS SABBATICAL

This is a ten-day retreat you take for yourself, with a task in mind. Write down ten positive talents or characteristics you have. Make an agreement with yourself to relax, but focus your creative imagination on ways to enhance that positive part of you, and make it more valuable, in a lazy day of contemplation. You will thus be taking one full day for each positive talent or characteristic. The ideas you come up with will be worth a hundred times any income you've lost during the ten days!

THE LAZINESS REWARD

Whenever you have made some goal, reached some new accomplishment, done something you're proud of, take a few days off to loaf and offer yourself some congratulations. After finishing a book, I always take a couple of days off in which I do absolutely nothing, not even think about any new book projects. Even in times when I was almost broke and had no idea when my next income would come in, I resisted the temptation to frantically go out and try to solve my financial problems. And I always found myself so refreshed after a couple of days of lying on sunny beaches that I was able to pour out an endless stream of valuable ideas on my return to productivity. You owe it to yourself to provide your creative mind with an opportunity to prove to you that loafing pays off, physically, emotionally, and financially.

Just in terms of health, you can't afford not to take it easier. The reason a number of large corporations brought me in to teach relaxation and meditation techniques was because their executives were dropping off like flies from stress diseases. Back in 1971 when I first started doing this training, corporations were just beginning to realize that it was costing them a fortune to replace people who didn't know how to take care of themselves. Learning to eliminate stress from your life can add five years onto the end of it. Even if you put yourself at a modest valuation such as $15,000 a year, that's $75,000 in income down the drain, not to count all the pleasures you could have in five years! So the next time someone asks you why you're loafing, just tell them, "I'm not loafing. I'm eliminating stress from my life, developing a lot of new valuable ideas, and giving myself a taste of the prosperity that's eventually coming to me!"

Some of the great achievers in history have

been basically lazy. To have the freedom of mind just to let go of goal orientation is a major human breakthrough. The creative mind needs a state of relaxed calm to really get going, and working hard is one way to deny and avoid your own creativity.

TRANSCEND GUILT

Loafing will stir up a lot of opposition from people who don't want you to have it easier than they. These poverty boosters will try to make you feel guilty. Since the creative loafer will be more relaxed, happier, and probably a lot richer than his neighbors, he's bound to produce some hostility. The best way to overcome this envy is to let them in on the secret. Creative Laziness is catching. Someone attending one of my seminars once asked me what would happen to the world if everyone just took it easy. I responded that it would be a much happier world, and a lot more would get done. Someone who has the ability to loaf, and the freedom to exercise that ability on a regular basis, has the kind of self-confidence that can scale any heights and succeed in any endeavor.

PROSPERITY PROCLAMATIONS

Three of the seven Prosperity Proclamations are especially suitable for WORKLOVE.

I HAVE AN UNLIMITED NUMBER OF VALUABLE IDEAS IN MY CONSCIOUS-NESS.

This will help you realize that the worst thing you could do for yourself is work at something you don't love, and refuse to give yourself the time you need to use those valuable ideas at a conscious state of awareness. As you use this affirmation, you'll find many of those ideas just popping into your head. Many great scientists and artists have reported that important ideas popped into their heads, sometimes just after making a statement like "I wish I could come up with an idea for this." Your subconscious mind is an obedient servant, if you give yourself the freedom to ask for what you really want. Loving yourself enough to acknowledge how creative you are is one of the best ways to lift your spirits and your income.

I LOVE WHAT I DO, AND THAT LOVE BRINGS ME ALL THE MONEY I WANT.

Of all the MONEYLOVE concepts, some people find it hardest to accept the fact that what you do is more important than how much you make, and how you feel about it is more important than what you do. Money achieves an unhealthy and abnormal importance in someone's life only when what they do fails to nourish, enthuse, and enliven them. If you work forty hours a week at a job that doesn't excite and pleasure you, then no matter how much money you are paid for that work, you won't be able to buy back a single one of those forty hours.

NO MATTER WHAT I DO, MY FINANCIAL WORTH INCREASES EVERY DAY.

This is one of the most potent of all the Prosperity Proclamations, since it directly reprograms a lot of negative conditioning to the effect that you are rewarded only for hard work. You are actually an income-producing property, and as such your value does increase every day. Beginning to realize this prosperity truth will help you build your self-esteem to the level where you can produce valuable ideas and income-producing methods whenever you desire. It's also a great affirmation for Creative Laziness. Understand this: There's no way working an eight-hour day can be as valuable to you as the new ideas a healthy loafing session will stimulate! And you'll know you've reached prosperity consciousness the day you can take a day off and tell everyone concerned you're going to loaf, rather than apologizing, lying, or making excuses!

These three Prosperity Proclamations can be valuable aids to your WORKLOVE efforts. In addition to taking some time out now to say them each twenty times, and write them each twenty times, prepare some cards with them printed carefully, and display them in areas where you'll be using your imagination to come up with prosperity ideas. They will encourage you and remind you of your own capacity for productive effort.

Remember, hard work is work without love. And when you work just for money, your imagination becomes a slave to money. You are free, a free person with free will, and the greatest expression of that freedom is simply to do what you want to do. You deserve *that* most of all!

3
And the Money Goes Round and Round

Once you have decided to keep a certain pile, it is no longer yours; for you can't spend it.
   —MONTAIGNE

Almost any man knows how to earn money, but not one in a million knows how to spend it.
   —HENRY DAVID THOREAU

I was originally going to call this chapter "Prosperity Spending," but then I started to examine the word *spend*, with all its negative connotations. The precise definition of *spend* is "consume or waste." I think that goes to the heart of a lot of poverty consciousness, the idea that when you use your money you are using it up, eliminating it, wasting it. While I don't really expect you to stop using the word, and, in fact, I probably will go on using it myself, since it's become such an ingrained part of common usage, it would do us all good to realize it has negative aspects that may affect our emotional attitudes toward the use of our money. Since I've started paying attention to this, as a result of planning this chapter, I find myself still using the word, but not as often, and with more awareness.

To check out its emotional impact for you, say the following sentences and experience how they make you feel:

"I've spent all my money."

"Let's spend it now!"

"I can't spend that."

The primary purpose of this chapter is to get you into the habit of thinking about money as a never-ending event, which goes and comes, but is always there. Money circulates. We, as individuals, have only temporary use of it, never full possession. To kid yourself that you possess money just because you have removed it from circulation is ludicrous and self-defeating. If our medium of exchange were apples instead of money, and you put thousands of apples away in a warehouse, instead of distributing them so you and others could enjoy them, you wouldn't be rich, you'd be poor. You'd be a poor person who happened to have a lot of apples rotting away in a warehouse! If all your money is tied up in the bank or investments, then you may as well be living on a desert island for all the good it does you.

The money goes round and round, and as it circulates it stimulates the economy, thus providing more opportunities for you to make more money. Extremely prosperous people have always realized this, which is why they spend and give away large amounts of money. It perhaps takes a bit more courage to use your money when you *don't* have a million dollars, but that courage will be repaid over and over again, if you obey certain money use laws. These commonsense rules include the following:

1. Keep track of the money you circulate.
2. Trust your feelings when confronted by a spending decision.
3. Never spend money without a sense of it as a medium of exchange, knowing full well what you are getting in return.
4. Balance your necessary expenses with pleasurable spending.
5. Experience your money as a current event, rather than as future purchasing power.
6. Love yourself enough to realize you deserve the best.
7. Remember: the more you savor what you buy, the more value you get for your money.
8. Realize that most of your days involve a positive cash flow.
9. Buy for yourself, not according to what others tell you.
10. Understand that if you have enough money to pay for it, you can afford it.
11. Clearly see that the more you enjoy using money, the more desire you will build to achieve prosperity.
12. Realize that feeling guilty about spending money indicates a lack of faith in your own capacity to create more.

Let's go over these twelve money use laws one by one.

1. KEEP TRACK OF THE MONEY YOU CIRCULATE.

The best way to do this is by keeping a record. Try keeping a MONEYLOVE JOURNAL. To make it a step beyond a mere tally of what comes in and what goes out, you can keep track of *how* you use it. I suggest you consider the following categories:

PLEASURE. This is money you exchange for good feelings. This can be in the form of a movie you've enjoyed, a dinner that was delicious, a visit to a friend, a book or vacation or long-distance telephone call that provided you with an enjoyable experience.

REGULAR BILLS. These are the rent, gas, electric, cleaning, and so on.

SPECIAL PURCHASE. This is anything that doesn't appear as a regular item in your budget: a new television set, a seminar you attend, a gift, a medical emergency.

DEBTS. This is any money you use to pay off financial obligations.

INVESTMENTS. Any money used to increase your net worth.

BANKING. Any money you put in the bank, for whatever purpose.

One good way to keep track of your money is to provide yourself with a survey month: one month in which you keep track of all your expenditures and figure out the percentages for each. Then you might draw a circle and divide up the various categories according to how much you spent for each. For instance:

As you can see, in this circle REGULAR BILLS is the single largest category. Paying off DEBTS is the smallest. PLEASURE comes in for a pretty fair share, along with BANKING. All in all, this is an example of some well-balanced money use.

To keep further track of your money, divide your REGULAR BILLS category into sub-groupings, such as rent, food, and utilities. You might then, after seeing how much you usually spend in a month on each item, make an effort to cut down a particular expenditure. For instance, food is an easy one to cut down.

Leonard Orr suggests the perfect way to save most of your food budget: Just get seven friends to invite you to dinner once a week each. Certainly you have some good friends who would enjoy your company for dinner. Part of your prosperity consciousness is believing you are interesting and worthwhile to be with. If you got just one person a week to invite you to lunch or dinner, you'd save some money in that part of your budget. The only budget item I don't suggest keeping close watch on is the PLEASURE section. You might vary and adjust the other categories, but it's important for your sense of money as a source of personal pleasure to keep this one intact, and even let it expand when that feels right.

A friend of mine really made a dent in his REGULAR BILLS section of the circle when he started house-sitting. He found that a lot of wealthy people left their homes for the summer months and were more than willing to pay a nominal fee to a dependable house-sitter and give him free room and board. He gave up his apartment and started house-sitting on a regular basis. It also developed his prosperity consciousness by exposing him to a wealthy life-style. By persistent investigation, he was able to line up wealthy vacationers throughout the year. If a few weeks were left open, he took his own vacations with the money he had saved on rent. If you use your creative imagination, you can play all sorts of games with your budget, and keeping track of your money will give you a valuable tool in this effort.

Playing with your budget also keeps it alive instead of a rigid set of habits. If you used 20 percent of your income last month for clothing, increase it to 50 percent this month. If you used 25 percent for food, lower it to 20 percent. Playing like this is one way to pay more attention to what you get for your money. And it will challenge your creative imagination. It may seem difficult to cut down on some budget items, and even harder to give yourself permission to expand others, but the practice it will give you in having a flexible attitude toward money will be priceless. Take yourself out of the realm of those statistical creatures who always spend such and such a percentage of their income for food, shelter, clothing, entertainment. Give yourself some provocative tasks, such as eliminating your expenses for food, clothing, and shelter for an entire month and spending that portion of your income on fun instead! I'm not suggesting you become totally irresponsible, merely more flexible and more spontaneous. The Self-actualized people Dr. Abraham Maslow researched also had spontaneity as one of their main personality traits. In many senses, they had the capacity of children who haven't yet learned to fear the ridicule and criticism of others, and are still able to see things freshly. Maslow said: "Almost any child can compose a song or poem or a dance or a painting or a play or a game on the spur of the moment, without planning or previous intent." So see if you can't have the beautifully fresh approach of a child to your budget.

2. TRUST YOUR FEELINGS WHEN CONFRONTED BY A SPENDING DECISION.

Inside you there is a barometer that can help you decide whether or not something is right for you. If you just take the time to relax and pay attention, you'll know at a gut level whether or not you really want to do something or buy something. Trust those feelings. Most people get into trouble when they use their analytical, logical-rational minds to make decisions on issues that have emotional impact. This creates a conflict between the left side of your brain, the rational, verbal side, and the right side of your brain, the creative, feeling side. In order to be prosperous, it's vital that you nourish the right side of your brain as much as possible, since it is this side's activities that are going to make you rich. Going against your feelings by saying such things as "I'll be sensible" is the most unsensible thing you can do. Trusting your gut feelings is a way you have of loving yourself. Check them out, by all means. Make certain you really feel you want to spend your money this way, that you really want what you'll be getting in exchange for your money, and then do it!

One of the great myths about money is

that it's a left-brain invention and you must use your analytical mind to deal with it. Money is a dream, one of the great abstract ideas of all time. This might be one of the core problems people have with money: assuming it is fact, when it's actually fancy; assuming it has a life of its own, when it has only the life you give it.

Your feelings come from your subconscious mind and are often signals being sent from your creative center to your conscious mind, signals containing messages on what it would be right for you to do at that particular moment. To deny those signals would be like shutting a door in the face of your subconscious. Enough of this, and the ideas will stop coming. And you will be bogged down in the kind of superficial conscious-mind-only thinking that will guarantee emotional, intellectual, and financial stagnation. So trust your feelings; they are your best friends!

3. NEVER SPEND MONEY WITHOUT A SENSE OF IT AS A MEDIUM OF EXCHANGE KNOWING FULL WELL WHAT YOU ARE GETTING IN RETURN.

It's fine to take money light and easy, but having a casual attitude about what you get in return for your money can be one of the ways to keep yourself in poverty consciousness! I don't mean making sure you get superior value for every dollar you spend like some emotionally retarded old miser, but I do mean having a sense of the quality you are buying. When you go to see a show that you love, have a sense of that love being provided in exchange for the money you used. When you learn something new, have a sense of that money being exchanged for knowledge. When you buy food, have a sense of the money circulating and bringing you back pleasant taste sensations and physical nourishment. If you spend money on an object that gives you no pleasure, and performs no useful service, and stimulates no new ideas, then you can consider your money exchanged for a poor bargain. The more positive exchange experiences you give yourself, the deeper your personal connection to prosperity. If you provide too many negative exchanges, your subconscious mind is going to get the message that money doesn't buy you much worthwhile, and it is therefore nonproductive for you to get rich!

One of these negative exchange experiences is buying solutions for painful circumstances with your money—spending it on illness and other emergencies. Of course, money can really come in handy when you're suffering. But if you designate a large amount of money for this purpose, then you have an imbalance in your *positive* ledger, which it is important to *increase*. A prime example of poverty consciousness is putting away money for illness or other emergencies. It's like the old joke about the two cowboys setting off on a trip. One notices the other carrying two paper bags and asks what they're for. The other replies, "This bag contains whiskey to be used for snakebite." The friend asks him what the second bag is for. He replies, "This one has the snake." Well, putting money away just for illness can turn your subconscious into the snake! Your subconscious mind can create illness. If you focus a lot of your energy on worrying about illness, to the extent that you earmark large sums of money toward it, as an obedient servant your subconscious may just assume you are preparing for illness and are ready to welcome it!

4. BALANCE YOUR NECESSARY EXPENSES WITH PLEASURABLE SPENDING.

This is self-explanatory. If you spend money only on things that are ordinary and mundane, your subconscious mind won't be very inspired to produce more money for you. Being wealthy takes imagination. Enjoying being wealthy takes even more. Many of the people who attend my MONEYLOVE seminars already have high incomes but are looking for ways to have more fun with them. One signal you can give your creative mind, instead of "How can I earn more money?," is "How can I have more fun?" After all, if you are asking for money so that you can have fun with it, why not directly ask for the fun and cut out the middleman: money. If you do this, the money will come anyway. You'll help it along by always earmarking a portion of your available funds for fun. You might even give them that title, FUNDS FOR FUN. I know some people reading this are going to be getting messages from their inner pauper advising that "there are no available funds for fun in your financial situation." Well, here's some news for you. That's a lie, a lie manufactured by your inner pauper to seduce you into continued poverty consciousness. You are in charge of your finances right now, no matter how little or how much you have. And you can use that money for whatever purposes you desire. Money doesn't have a mind of its own. It's no coincidence that for so many people their expenses seem to expand to meet their earnings. That's the result of saying you have no money for fun. Your subconscious mind, again the obedient servant, will listen to the message that your money is going only toward food, shelter, and other necessities and deliver enough of those necessities to use up all your money. Put a stop to that, right now! Take five dollars, or ten dollars, and blow it on yourself! It can be the most valuable investment you'll ever make in your future success.

5. EXPERIENCE YOUR MONEY AS A CURRENT EVENT, RATHER THAN AS FUTURE PURCHASING POWER.

Money *is* a current event. It has life only now. When you are really prosperous, you can afford to put away something that's alive now for the unforeseen future. But until you get there, until you have more money than you know what to do with, using it now makes the most sense. If you want to go into the economics of it, just realize that we'll probably always live in an inflationary cycle, so that your money put away and taken out for exchange ten years from now will never buy you then what you could have bought right now. Fear causes many people to make the foolish mistake of thinking their money will buy them more tomorrow than it does today. That's how people drop dead at an early age with lots of money in the bank and no smiles on their faces. I've had people say to me, "I'm glad I put away money for my old age, because now that I'm on in years, I can live comfortably." I think those people are trying to convince themselves; they're certainly not convincing anyone else that they're happy about their current situation. They made a poor bargain trading in the present for the future, and they're stuck with it. I'd like to share a thought with you now, that *if you can believe it* may save your life! That thought is simply this:

PUTTING AWAY MONEY FOR YOUR OLD AGE WILL GUARANTEE THAT YOU'LL GET OLD.

Sending signals to your subconscious mind that a good deal of your money is being put away for the day when you are so old and incapacitated you no longer can earn money will hasten that day. Your subconscious, always eager to provide you with the circumstances in which you can spend your money, will deliver those circumstances! Look around at the elderly people who are still youthful, and ask *them* if they sacrificed current pleasure for future comfort. Then ask those who are sour-faced, depressed, and bent over. I feel pretty confident that your research will bear me out, will emphasize the futility of saving for your old age.

6. LOVE YOURSELF ENOUGH TO REALIZE YOU DESERVE THE BEST.

Economizing can create a "poor me" attitude toward finances and all other facets of your life. You do deserve to wear good clothes, eat good food, live in a well-furnished and attractive environment, travel first class, buy the best-made products, and do all of the things supposedly reserved for people of extreme wealth. You may have to do it in moderation, and your one good outfit may replace three or four not-so-fine selections, but it will be more than worth it in terms of your self-image.

I learned a valuable lesson when I was working at NBC, and earning a lot of money, back in 1970. I bought very good clothes then. When I left broadcasting to concentrate my efforts on developing the techniques that eventually led to this book, I had a substantially reduced income. It would have been difficult for me to go out and buy even modestly priced clothes. But I didn't have to do that, because the expensive, finely made clothes I had in my closet lasted. And lasted and lasted and lasted! I still have most of them. By all means be a careful shopper, not to "save" money, but to make sure when you pay for the best that you get the best. Don't fall victim to merchants who mistake high prices for quality. I have found some superb fashions in discount men's stores, and women's shops offer even more of a variety. The point is not to worry about the cost when you find something you really want. Practice developing this habit by going out to buy something and shopping without looking at the price tag. Just pick out what you want, and decide to get it on the basis of whether you like it, rather than on the basis of cost.

A word about bargain hunting. If you get a kick out of it, fine. But understand that you may be feeding your subconscious some poverty messages when you get excited about saving a few dollars. Another valuable lesson I learned from my mother was the result of her using the term "Penny wise, pound foolish" to describe someone who wasted a whole day shopping around to save two dollars on something.

Restaurants are places where a lot of people do themselves in in terms of personal pettiness. Get in the habit of knowing the price range at restaurants you frequent, especially the highest-priced item on the menu. Don't go unless you are willing to spend that much. And when you go, don't look at the right-hand side of the menu. If you are ready to be more adventurous, do this at a new restaurant. Settling for less than the most delicious meal you can order, to save a few dollars, is like swallowing poison in terms of what it is doing to your subconscious mind, that marvelous instrument you must depend on to earn you a fortune!

7. THE MORE YOU SAVOR WHAT YOU BUY, THE MORE VALUE YOU GET FOR YOUR MONEY.

The more intensely you experience what you are buying, the more value you are getting for your money. What makes a life most valuable is the quality of time used. The healthiest and happiest way to use your money is in exchange for something that can provide you with many alive moments of sensory pleasure, fully engaging your mind, your body, and your emotions. How sad it is seeing someone focus attention on how much money he or she "saved" in contrast to the joy of someone enjoying with great delight what their money brought them! I particularly remember going on a seashore vacation with some friends. I gladly paid six dollars more a night to have an ocean-view room. They opted for the economy side of the hotel. Just the time they spent coming over to my room to watch the view more than made up for the difference in price! And at some subconscious level they had to feel pretty cheap. But at least they were able to appreciate the view. In order to justify their "economies" many people shut off their senses so that they won't be confronted with what they are missing.

8. REALIZE THAT MOST OF YOUR DAYS INVOLVE A POSITIVE CASH FLOW.

Positive cash flow. Doesn't that have a nice sound to it? It can conjure up a vision of rivers of money flowing toward you. And you already have it! Every day that more money comes into your life than goes out, you are operating with a positive cash flow. Most people do themselves in psychologically by counting only the end results of their monthly transactions. If, for instance, you pay all your bills on one day at the end or beginning of the month, you have a positive cash flow the other twenty-nine or thirty days! And it's not just kidding yourself, it's really understanding the economics of your financial life. If today you earned $35, and you spent only $20, even if you owe $150 in immediate bills you still have a positive cash flow of $15, if you haven't actually mailed out those payments. This is the kind of positive reinforcement your prosperity consciousness loves. *If wealth is an attitude, as most experts seem to agree, then working on your attitude is the way to get wealthy.*

You never do yourself any good by imagining that more money is going out than coming in. Even if, at the end of the month, this is temporarily true, focus instead on the positive cash flow you have most of the days of your life. Amounts aren't as important as the fact that *more days* see money coming in than see money going out. Close your eyes for a moment. Yes, right now. Just close them, and envision what your life is like with a positive cash flow. Did you find it hard to accept? Well, if you start telling yourself MORE MONEY IS COMING IN THAN GOING OUT MOST OF THE DAYS OF MY LIFE, you'll very clearly begin to see an effect. You may even want to adopt this as another Prosperity Proclamation.

9. *BUY FOR YOURSELF, NOT ACCORDING TO WHAT OTHERS TELL YOU.*

This is a touchy issue for some people. Our parents often gave us advice to buy certain things in a certain way, and we still have some remnants of those old money messages. For instance, my mother always suggested waiting for sales. For a long time I would hold off buying something I wanted until it was on sale. And sometimes I just never got it. Now I consider my time too valuable to look for sales. If an item's on sale, great, I see nothing wrong with buying something you want, when you want it, at a lower price. But spending time and energy to follow those old money messages is ridiculous. Others will also tell you where to shop, what specific products to buy, and how much you should spend. Accepting good advice is common sense, but allowing others to make all your choices robs you of one of your basic freedoms: the freedom to learn for yourself.

Couples often have problems with money, and we're told that it accounts for a lot of divorces. One of the obstacles to good couple finances is the putting of all the money earned by both people into one pile. Hostility can then be built up when the man wants to buy a camera, and the woman wants to buy a clothes dryer, and the debate starts over how *"you're* going to spend *our* money." When counseling couples on money matters, I suggest that each of them have a specific amount each month as PERSONAL PLEASURE MONEY, over and above their joint banking accounts and daily living expenses. For instance, one woman I know has now delegated $100 a month for her own personal use out of the joint family money pile. She plans all sorts of pleasurable experiences for herself. And she doesn't feel badly, as she once did, when her husband decides to spend money on one of his interests. The liberation of the American woman from traditional stereotyped roles is helping to overcome this problem. But this hasn't always filtered down to money. For instance, many a woman who considers herself otherwise liberated expects the man to pay for dinner when they are dating—even if she earns as much or more than he does! This clinging to ancient tribal customs is destructive to both parties. It perpetuates the woman's poverty consciousness belief that she will never earn as much as men, or that she must be dependent on a man. It also perpetuates the man's poverty consciousness belief that women must be taken care of and protected, since they can't do it themselves. I got in touch with this about six years ago when I was dating a woman earning about twice my income. Now, I could easily afford to pay for dinner, *but so could she!* She was so rooted in poverty consciousness that she took it for granted that I would pay. I just couldn't see how my buying dinner for someone who could well afford to buy me dinner made me a better person. This became even more ludicrous when I was struggling along on almost no income at all and dating woman who were professionals earning twenty to forty thousand dollars a year. Some of them were still so caught up in their old programming that they would develop galloping anxiety attacks if I so much as suggested we go dutch. Understand, I love treating someone to dinner, as a special event, as a gift. But *not* because it's expected of me, and *not* because the other person feels uncomfortable doing it any other way.

I took some of these feelings into the heart of liberation land when I addressed a meeting of the National Organization of Women. I said, "How come you women feel liberated when you go dutch with a man, but hardly ever feel liberated enough to pay the whole bill?" This got me a fascinating response: four dinner invitations!

10. UNDERSTAND THAT IF YOU HAVE ENOUGH MONEY TO PAY FOR IT, YOU CAN AFFORD IT.

I talked about this a bit in the first chapter. I said there that "I can't afford it" is often a lie, almost always an untruth. To take it a step further, you are doing powerful damage to your subconscious mind, your marvelous money machine, every time you feed in the negative programming "I can't afford it." Again, your subconscious will accept imagined fact as readily as real fact. If you say "I can't afford it" enough times, you will become a person who *really* can't afford it.

What a lot of people who say "I can't afford it" are really saying is "I don't deserve it." This is not to suggest that you splurge on things that you don't need. But pay attention whenever you are about to say "I can't afford it." See whether you aren't really making a statement to the effect that this isn't how you are willing to use your money. I often use a little exercise in my workshop, asking people to list a series of things they can't do. Each sentence must start with the words "I can't." One such list looked like this:

"I can't fly."

"I can't buy a new car."

"I can't find someone to love."
"I can't seem to get ahead."
"I can't understand this exercise."

I then suggest that each person change all the "I can't" statements to "I won't," so the same list would look like this:

"I won't fly."
"I won't buy a new car."
"I won't find someone to love."
"I won't seem to get ahead."
"I won't understand this exercise."

Try this for yourself. Not only now in the form of an exercise, but in your life, whenever confronted by an "I can't" statement. "I can't afford it" then becomes "I won't afford it," and this will give your subconscious mind the important idea that you are in charge of your own life. "I can't do it" is negative thinking, while "I won't do it" is a choice you're making. I know this sounds very simplistic, but if you use it you'll begin to see some changes in the way you feel about yourself.

One of the silliest things people say is "I can't afford it, but I'm going to do it anyway." It's as if they need to remind themselves they're being foolish. Much better to say, "I thought I couldn't afford it, but I decided it was important to give this to myself."

This situation can be tremendously clarified if you use THE POVERTY PENALTY. If you fine yourself a hundred dollars every time you say "I can't afford it," you won't be able to afford to keep saying it. And that hundred dollars *has* to be spent on pleasure.

First impressions create a certain mindset that is difficult to erase. Have you ever noticed, as an example of this, that if someone you are meeting for the first time is wearing glasses, you always think of that person as someone who wears glasses, even if he or she never wears them again? While someone who wears glasses often may not be considered as such if he or she wasn't wearing them the first time you met. Saying "I can't afford it" over and over again will create the impression that you can't afford it, and this will be difficult to overcome even when you have lots of money. This is one reason some wealthy people get no pleasure out of spending their money.

11. CLEARLY SEE THAT THE MORE YOU ENJOY USING MONEY, THE MORE DESIRE YOU WILL BUILD TO ACHIEVE PROSPERITY.

If your sophisticated computer brain gets a lot of information to the effect that money creates hassles, that money is linked with difficulty, that money and anxiety go hand in hand, that money is for buying security instead of pleasure, then your subconscious mind will keep you from getting a lot more money. But if you circulate your money with love and joy, and a sense that life is worth living and money worth spending, then your internal moneymaking machine will go full steam ahead. It's really sad how many people of means think they'll be able to relax and someday *start* enjoying their money. But waiting until you have a certain amount to start enjoying it is like waiting for a paycheck before you start to look for a job. It just may be too late to *get* started. I've had many very rich people come to my seminars, and come to me for private consultations, and without exception I've found that their main problem was waiting too long to start enjoying their success. They were often on a perpetual motion machine when making their money, and just found it terribly hard to get off and take a vacation. I think every bill of every denomination ought to have engraved on it:

THIS BILL IS FOR PLEASURE. NOT ENJOYING IT MAY BE HAZARDOUS TO YOUR EMOTIONAL HEALTH.

Many people are future-oriented, but the MONEYLOVE concept is to enjoy your wealth as it is happening, so you love the process as much as the goal. Every dollar you receive is an opportunity to learn more about money, to learn more about enjoying using your money, and an opportunity to build that clear vision of what you want. Abstract concepts can be very potent, but money in a bank, or locked away, is too abstract a concept for the most imaginative person to translate into financial satisfaction or financial independence. You've got to play with your money, touch your money, and use your money, in order to become money-conscious.

12. REALIZE THAT FEELING GUILTY ABOUT SPENDING MONEY INDICATES A LACK OF FAITH IN YOUR OWN CAPACITY TO CREATE MORE.

Feeling guilty about circulating money has nothing to do with how much money you have to circulate. There are millionaires who feel guilt every time they spend five dollars on themselves. By dealing with money in terms of figures transferred from one set of books to another, rather than physically handling it, many wealthy people have a deep disbelief in their prosperity. This prevents them from eliminating the fear of poverty that is such a part of their inner awareness. Statements such as: "If I spend this much this foolishly, I will suffer"; "I have a limited amount, so I'd better hold on to what I've got"; "This money should be used to help others instead of giving me pleasure" are all poverty-conscious statements.

The last of the above negative statements may strike a particular chord in you. Many people who give away a lot of money are operating on the basis of guilt. True generosity of spirit is motivated by a much healthier outlook. It's much more honest to use your money for pleasure than to give it away pretending you don't expect something in return, whether it be recognition here on earth or some sense of reward in heaven. The same human laws apply to giving as do to working: The more you love what you are doing, the more successful it will be for you. If you want to give your money away, give it to people who are doing something you respect, who are working on a project you are enthusiastic about. Absentee giving is a way of dehumanizing the exchange of money. For instance, your time is often a much better gift than your money, a more effective and more real form of generosity. The greatest way to express your prosperity consciousness is to give your money to someone who really doesn't need it, just because you like what they're doing. Quite often, giving money to fill a desperate need merely feeds that neediness, expanding the desperation and preventing those involved from using their creative imaginations to fill their need. Also, this is a very important truth: GIVING MONEY AWAY ONLY TO THOSE WHO NEED IT WILL REINFORCE THE POVERTY BELIEF THAT YOU WILL GET MONEY ONLY WHEN YOU NEED IT. Prosperity is going beyond mere need to a surplus economy. If you want to do more than survive, then keep this in mind, and give with love, a sense of sharing surplus, and an understanding that what you are giving is just pieces of paper, just a symbol. What matters is what is done with those pieces of paper.

A word here about tithing: I don't tithe myself, but many people whose opinions I respect have reported great success in their lives, success they directly attribute to freely giving a tenth of their income to some spiritual work, whether it be a religious or a secular organization. It is an ancient tradition observed in many lands to give a tenth of what you earn to the work of God. In the reports of tithing I've received, most of the people started tithing before they achieved substantial wealth, at a time when it could have been easily argued that they couldn't afford to give up a tenth of their income. But without exception they say that they learned to get more out of the remaining 90 percent than they had out of the total amount, and that their income started increasing almost immediately.

One thing tithing certainly does is help increase your feeling of prosperity. Feeling you are prosperous enough to give up a tenth of your income may indeed stimulate your creative imagination to the point where you more than make up the difference. But don't tithe just to gain, my friends tell me, do it because you appreciate your many gifts, and because you want to share the fruits of your labor. It also seems to be important not to make tithing conditional or a future promise, such as, "When I'm successful, I will tithe."

As I said, I don't tithe, but I've heard enough stories of the power of this tradition not to rule out starting someday soon. If you give money away, allow it to be in a manner that will enhance your prosperity consciousness and sense of well-being.

PROSPERITY PROCLAMATION

The Prosperity Proclamation that is specifically geared toward the use, exchange, and circulation of your money is:

EVERY DOLLAR I CIRCULATE ENRICHES THE ECONOMY AND COMES BACK TO ME MULTIPLIED.

All the tools contained in this chapter, every word of the money use laws, are aimed at helping you accept this Prosperity Proclamation at an emotional level of consciousness. Once you do that, you'll have no trouble enjoying your money to the fullest. It will no longer be a question of "I can't afford that," but will instead become a question of "Do I really want that?"

Write the Prosperity Proclamation on money circulation twenty times, and say it twenty times before going on to the next chapter.

Learning to say yes to your money will enable you to say yes to yourself, and that will make you the kind of person other people will want to say yes to.

One final idea: Have this proclamation printed on your checks. You'll be amazed how much more pleasant paying bills will become!

4
Prosperity
Banking

*Taking it all in all, I find it is more trouble
to watch after money than to get it.*
  —Montaigne

*A banker is a fellow who lends his umbrella
when the sun is shining and wants it back the
minute it begins to rain.*
  —Mark Twain

A cartoon shows a simply dressed couple standing in front of a modern palace of banking, dwarfed by its shining marble façade. The man says to the woman, "Somehow, dear, an old sock seems more appropriate." Well, I have news for you: Despite their often overwhelming architecture, despite the sometimes patronizing and intimidating attitude of their employees, and despite the bureaucratic hurdles one has to overcome in order to do business with them, the nation's multibillion-dollar banking institutions are a valuable tool that can move you toward financial satisfaction and financial independence!

HOW DO YOU FEEL ABOUT BANKS?

Before exploring the many benefits you can gain from Prosperity Banking, it's important to examine your current attitudes and where they came from. Finish the sentence "For me, putting money in the bank means_____

————." Your answer may give you an idea of how you view banks in general. Part of this is a reflection of your actual banking experience, and part of it has probably been influenced by your parents and significant others in your early life. I remember, for example, my grandfather's telling how he lost all the money he had in the bank when it closed during the depression. I'm certain this determined how he felt about banks for the next thirty-five years of his life. I know it affected my mother, and me in turn. For a good number of years I kept most of my money in my checking account and hardly any in a savings account. I would say, "I can't afford to put money in the bank right now." What a negative programming trip I was laying on myself! That was a ridiculous attitude. A much healthier approach would have been to say, "Right now, I have other priorities, and I'm choosing not to put any money in the bank." I could easily have afforded to put a dollar a week in a savings account, and sometimes even five dollars, without depriving myself in any way. Probably another negative banking myth that affected my actions in those days was the one that says you have to put big chunks of money in a bank for it to amount to anything. My career as a newsman provided me with a lot of insight into that myth. Often, for a human-interest story, I would cover the death of some poor derelict who was on welfare or had never earned more than a few dollars a week. The derelict would be found in bed, in a messy, terribly depressing room, with $80,000 stuffed into the mattress. These poor unfortunates were, of course, fanatics when it came to saving money. They were practicing miser consciousness rather than prosperity consciousness. They also all seemed to have an oppressive fear of banks. But I think we can learn a lesson from their misfortune: In terms of banking, *consistency is more important than quantity*.

Another factor that may inhibit healthy banking attitudes is the subconscious fear that once you put your money in, you won't be able to withdraw it without a lot of hassle, or without having to explain what you want it for. This fear can prevent you from feeling free to withdraw money for frivolous reasons, an important freedom to have in terms of prosperity consciousness.

HOW DID YOUR PARENTS FEEL ABOUT BANKS?

Can you see any connection between what your parents believed about banks, and how you now feel on the subject? For instance:

Did your parents consider going to the bank a solemn or joyful experience?

Did they withdraw money only for tragic emergencies?

Did they feel free to take out money to splurge on some pleasure for themselves or you?

Did they trust the bank to take good care of their money?

If one or both of your parents are still alive, you might chat with them about banks and banking and find out their basic attitudes. Once you can see where some of your negative programming originated, you can flow forward and develop a program of using banks creatively for your own financial benefit.

Another helpful device in overcoming some of the current emotional impact of that old negative conditioning is to start avoiding the words *save* and *savings* when referring to money in the bank. To say you are "saving" your money conjures up an image of rescuing it from a fate worse than death. And that fate may merely be spending money on something pleasurable or useful for yourself. The words are just too involved with symbols and images that get in the way of prosperity consciousness. Check out, for example, what you feel when you see or hear the old aphorism "A penny saved is a penny earned." Does this make you jump for joy and feel good about banking? Or does it remind you of an authority figure telling you how to run your life? I'm not saying that the advice isn't true, just that it's too strongly connected to old attitudes about banking. The word *banking* also has more of a feel of wealth and financial independence about it. Poor people save their money, rich people bank it. So, from now on, you are banking your money.

YOUR SEVEN PROSPERITY BANKING ACCOUNTS

Why seven bank accounts? Because, from now on, you are going to use banks to foster in you a self-image of a person of means and substance. It's pretty hard to see yourself as a loser with seven bank accounts. And each one has a very specific purpose. In fact, once you achieve an initial goal, you'll be adding an eighth account!

These seven accounts will help you to keep track of your money and to have a sense of direction and financial purpose.

Just shopping around for seven banks will be an adventure that will build your prosperity consciousness. Maintain high standards. After all, you *are* an important customer, and will become even more important as your Prosperity Banking system begins to work. Don't choose any bank where you are not made to feel welcome, or where the service is impolite or inefficient. This would merely reinforce any negative banking attitudes on your part. Choose attractive banks, with warm, attractive employees. If you want to add to the adventure of it, ask to see a bank officer and explain the purpose of the specific account you are going to open there. Also explain that you are starting out with a minimal amount to see how you are treated, and expect to become a major depositor in the coming years. Tell the officer that you are on the way to becoming financially independent, and you want to pick a bank where you'll feel comfortable and well served. And believe it as you say it, for it's really true. Once you started reading this book, you put yourself on the path to financial independence!

1. CASH FLOW ACCOUNT

This is the account into which you put your entire earnings or paycheck as soon as they are received. The basic rule is to leave it all in this account for at least twenty-four hours. If possible, leave it in for an entire month. This is all your income, and the idea is to have to go to the bank and withdraw what you need for everyday expenses. This will give you a much clearer idea of how you spend your money. The best way to do it is to keep it in the bank for a month, figure out what your expenses are for that month, and see if you can't manage on a little less. All surplus can be removed and placed in one of your other accounts at the end of the month. By leaving all your cash flow in the bank for at least twenty-four hours after receiving it, you'll begin to find you can survive without money. If you can go a day without taking from your income, it will be a major accomplishment in your MONEYLOVE training. You'll be amazed at what this Cash Flow Account will teach you about money, and how easy it will be to arrive at the end of the month with a surplus. If, for instance, you use the MONEYLOVE suggestion to have a friend invite you to dinner, you won't have to withdraw the money you would have needed for that meal. If you get four friends each to invite you once a month, as suggested in the last chapter, you'll start having a fat surplus every month—certainly enough to do something nice for your generous friends and still have quite a bit left over. Using your creative budgeting skills in conjunction with this account will automatically provide you with a new sense of personal wealth.

The main purpose of your Cash Flow Account is to give you a real sense of how cash flows in and out of your life, and give you an easy and direct means of changing that flow.

2. CREATIVE CONSUMER ACCOUNT

This is an account you go to for all major purchases. This may mean a vacation trip, a new TV, a car, a medical emergency, or a new camera. The basic rule is that you have to have a specific large purchase in mind, knowing that you will buy that item when you have enough money in this account. Another rule is that you have to work toward keeping this account empty. You are always aiming at getting enough money in the account so you can take it out and make your purchase. This may not be as easy as it sounds. When you start putting prosperity consciousness into practice, you may find that, as soon as you have enough money in the account, enough comes in from another source to pay for that particular item, or someone gives you what you were going to buy. This happened to me when I was saving for a dictation machine. I almost had enough in the bank, in my Creative Consumer Account, when lo and behold, a friend of mine who's a therapist called me up to tell me that a patient had run out of money and had paid for his therapy sessions with an almost-new dictation machine. My friend asked if I had any use for it, as he had no need or room for it. I took it off his hands with the agreement that we would split the profits if I ever sold it. This left me with about $400 in my Creative Consumer Account. So I decided to splurge and flew down to Nassau for an afternoon, just to play blackjack in the casino there. I had wanted to do this for quite a while, but hadn't felt I could afford it, and I firmly believe in never gambling unless I am ready, willing, and able to lose my entire stake. This also added to my prosperity consciousness, since the casinos are filled with wealthy people, and have an aura of prosperity. Just telling the immigration people that I had no luggage and had just flown in for the afternoon gave me the feeling of being a multi-millionaire. Even if I had lost it all, I think it would have been worth it. But I ended up almost doubling my money. So now I had about $700. I put $600 in my Financial Independence Account, since it was, in effect, found money, and I gave the rest to a friend who was collecting funds to bring a spiritual master over from India. This is the kind of thing that's always happening to me with MONEYLOVE. That old saying "When it rains, it pours" really makes sense when you are working on your prosperity consciousness, and the Creative Consumer Account can help you keep track of your major purchases, as well as stimulate your imagination.

3. FINANCIAL INDEPENDENCE ACCOUNT

This single account can do it all for you! Into this account you put only money you will not have to touch. Once you put money into your Financial Independence Account, it stays there. This is your one permanent bank account. Once you start this account, you are on the way to financial independence, for you have begun to accept it as a reality, and have actually started the process. There is one further stipulation that is an important part of the process. Remember, you are not only putting money away, but becoming more aware of your prosperity potential. To help you do this, arrange to have the interest paid to you by mail quarterly. You will probably have to have this account in a Savings and Loan Association in order to arrange this service. And your first goal is to have enough money in your Financial Independence Account to produce an interest check that will support you comfortably for one whole day. When that happens, you will have achieved partial financial independence, you will be financially independent four days a year! This will reinforce your determination and give you a taste of what it will be like when you can live without having to earn an income. You will be achieving financial independence one day at a time, the most emotionally healthy way to do it. It will begin to be a current event for you, rather than some far-off distant wish.

One important note, here, is to avoid becoming compulsive. The idea of financial independence may appeal to you so much that you'll rush to put money in this account that really doesn't belong in it, money you may need for other things, money you could be enjoying now. Remember, this is the money you can afford to put away indefinitely, after everything else is taken care of. It can start out small, as can all the Prosperity Banking Accounts, perhaps with as little as ten dollars in it. It's the idea that's important, the idea of getting started, of triggering the momentum. Getting to the point where your interest will support you for a day could take a year or more. In fact, there is an advantage in not putting enough in at the beginning to achieve that first goal: You can then enjoy the anticipation of reaching it, and more intensely experience the excitement of arriving at your first plateau on the road to financial independence!

4. SABBATICAL ACCOUNT

This account is designed for one special purpose: to give you enough money to take a year off. I can't stress too much the importance of having the idea of a sabbatical as a part of your prosperity consciousness. It gives you a specific, fairly short-range purpose, one that is more immediately achievable than complete financial independence. And it prepares you for the exciting possibilities of freedom from having to earn a living. Rather than counting the money in this account, count the days. For example, if it costs you thirty dollars a day to live comfortably, as soon as you have thirty dollars in this account you have the first day of your sabbatical.

The easiest way to make this work is to put 10 percent of your income into the account. With accumulating interest, it should take you about seven years to reach your goal. Actually, in practice, prosperity consciousness will get that account filled up even more quickly, and you may find yourself able to take a year off in as little as two or three years.

Taking 10 percent of your income may seem difficult, but it's easier than it appears. You can consider it as a form of tithing. Many people of very modest means manage to give 10 percent of their earnings to a church, so you could manage to give that amount to your Sabbatical Account. And if you want to add a more loving quality to the concept, make an agreement with yourself to spend some of your sabbatical year in giving service to others. One real estate salesman I know decided to spend a couple of weeks of his year reading to the blind. Another self-tither spent some of her sabbatical visiting old-age homes and just talking to some of the lonely people stashed away by relatives and a society too busy to care. She was fascinated with the interesting stories told by these men and women whom no one else would listen to—so fascinated, in fact, that she decided to write a book on the subject. It's just possible that when that book is finished and gets published she'll be able to take another year off. Giving freely, honestly, and with love can produce some amazing dividends. It also adds to your prosperity consciousness, since you begin to see yourself as someone who can afford to give to others.

As with your Financial Independence Account, it's important that you put in the Sabbatical Account only money that you absolutely don't need or want right now. Do not sacrifice current pleasure for future security. That's a very poor bargain.

The reason for having both a Financial Independence Account *and* a Sabbatical Account is to expand your prosperity alternatives. Moving toward both complete financial independence and temporary financial freedom for a year will give you two fiscal projects you have actually started, each of which can produce pleasant tingles of anticipation, each of which can give you a satisfying sense of accomplishment, and each of which can provide you with great financial rewards. The core concept here, as with all the MONEYLOVE techniques, is to reprogram your brain with a new way of thinking, while moving practically in a creative, productive, and prosperous direction.

5. PLEASURE ACCOUNT

Though all of your Prosperity Banking Accounts may give you pleasure in one form or another, this one will challenge you to come up with new ways to enjoy your money. Every penny in this account must be spent for your personal pleasure. And you can't let money accumulate here for more than three months. Every ninety days, you must empty the account and spend all the money on pleasure, on having a good time. This will allow you to learn even more deeply the basic truth that money is for pleasure. You'll have to keep a close watch on this account and make certain you aren't neglecting it in favor of the others. It's as vital to your future prosperity as your Financial Independence Account. Many people have put together huge fortunes and never gotten a moment's pleasure out of them. They had forgotten how to enjoy in their frantic effort to accumulate. Prosperity is not only having money, it is enjoying it!

The idea for the Pleasure Account came

from a story I heard told in Miami a few years ago by Dr. Leo Buscaglia, author of *Love* and *Personhood*. Leo told about an uncle of his who had died and left sums of money to each of his nieces and nephews, with the stipulation that the money had to be spent on pleasure, otherwise it would go to charity. You can imagine how this upset Leo's old-fashioned Italian mother, whose first inclination was probably to rush to the bank and put the money away for "the future." But the uncle's will had her trapped. If the money wasn't spent for fun, it had to go to charity. Imagine what that household was like, with eleven boys and girls, all with legacies they had to splurge on themselves, which was totally against everything Mama had taught them about money. What a way to instantly boost their prosperity consciousness!

There's another lesson in the rest of the story, as Leo Buscaglia tells it. "My definition of 'fun' at the time was to go and sit at the feet of Jean-Paul Sartre and live with the existentialists in Paris. My dad and my mother said, 'You can't go, my God, you're only sixteen years old!' So, after much ado, I said, 'I'll send it to charity! I'll give it to charity!' They said, 'Oh, you can't give it to charity, you've got to use it! Okay, go, but the minute you go, you have declared yourself independent of us.' Sure, I was ready. I get my money, and I get my little old suitcase, and off I go to Paris. The first thing, the *American in Paris* syndrome, I get a little garret apartment that

looks over all the little chimneytops. I buy
wood for the fireplace. I buy French wine and
Camembert cheese. And I invite all the people
in, and we rap all night about matters of con-
sequence. We don't know what the hell we're
talking about, but we're having such a good
time doing it! And, all of a sudden, in a bleak
November in Paris—and there is no bleaker
thing than a November in Paris, it is so cold
you cannot envision it—I realize I have no
more money. My rent is paid to the end of
the month, but that's it. No more wood, and
just a handful of coins. So I figure, 'Oh hell,
Mom is a soft touch, I'm going to let her
know. She won't let me die!' So I go and send
a telegram, the cheapest one I could send:
STARVING—LEO. Twenty-four hours later,
and I still have the telegram, I got the response: STARVE—MAMA!"

That was a moment of truth for Leo Buscaglia. But he survived. He got pretty hungry,
but he survived, and stayed in Paris another
year. One way to look at his experience, for
someone in poverty consciousness, is that he
had to pay for his pleasure with a lot of suffering. But that's not the way Leo looked at it.
He remembers it all as one of the most exciting, joyful, alive, and important learning
periods of his life. And he cites the despair
of hunger as one of the experiences that taught
him the most. In fact, after that telegram, a
year later, he went home and told his mother,
"Thank you, you made all the difference." Leo
was lucky. How many times do people post-

pone pleasure for fear of an outcome far less traumatic than going hungry in a bleak November in Paris? Far too many times, I'm afraid. Poverty consciousness is an insidious force in our culture and dictates that one must always be afraid of spending money for pleasure instead of for some "serious" purpose. The willingness to take a risk, to face up to any fears that have you resisting the enjoyment of money, is a major prerequisite for prosperity consciousness. Unwillingness to take that risk is a sign of poor self-esteem, in effect a statement that says you don't believe you deserve pleasure, and that you don't have the faith in your own creative talent that will let you believe you can easily replace any money you spend. The Pleasure Account is one way to start programming yourself to enjoy. It is a vital counterbalance to the other accounts and will ensure that the joyful part of you will win in the tug-of-war with the inner pauper in your personality.

6. INVESTMENT ACCOUNT

This is one of the simplest accounts of all. You put in only money that you can afford to invest. You take out money only when you find an investment that fills all the criteria cited in the following chapter, "Prosperity Investing," and one that will give you a return greater than the interest the bank is paying you.

7. MILLION-DOLLAR ACCOUNT

The only difference between you and someone who has a million dollars in the bank is all those zeros in the millionaire's bankbook. You are going to bridge that separation with the greatest of ease. Open an account for ten dollars, and write or type five extra zeros in your bankbook, so that it reads $1,000,000, and so that you can now see what it feels like to have a million dollars in the bank. This may seem silly to you, but it's a fact that the more you visualize something as being true, the easier it is to accept at an emotional level. The more you see yourself as wealthy, the easier it will be for you to overcome any emotional resistance connected to your poverty programming. You don't touch your Million-Dollar Account, it just sits there. You can pretend to yourself that, for some reason, you cannot touch the million dollars just yet. If you can begin to consider yourself as actually having a million dollars in the bank, it will begin to change your money attitudes. Not that you'll go out and blow $300,000 on a yacht, but you probably won't hesitate to spend fifteen dollars on a good dinner. After all, when you actually do accumulate a million dollars, that euphoria you will experience is a feeling you are creating. You are allowing the knowledge of a fortune to trigger a pleasant emotional reaction. And you are in charge of that trigger right now! The feeling of well-being is one you can create at this moment, and the

Million-Dollar Account is a tool to help you in that effort. It's an adult toy, if you will, one you can have fun playing with and use to learn some more about your money attitudes.

THE OPULENCE ACCOUNT

This is purposely not one of your seven original accounts. It's designed to be created only after you reach a specific goal with all your other accounts. You can choose the goal, but doubling the original amount in all seven might be a good guideline. You Opulence Account is just that, and the money in it is to be withdrawn regularly and used only to give you a taste of wealth. This means you must spend it on something you wouldn't have normally done, something you feel it takes a rich person to do. This may be renting a Rolls-Royce and a chauffeur for a day, going to a $100-a-plate charity dinner, flying to an island for the weekend, shopping in an exclusive shop, buying custom-made clothes, or giving an expensive gift to a friend. The main thing is to enjoy this conspicuous consumption and see what you can learn from it. You may learn that you really don't have to be rich to do some of these things. You may learn that some of these aren't as desirable as you thought they were. Most of all, you'll begin to feel a little more prosperous and plan to spend at least some of your money in the way an extremely wealthy person would. It's still another preparation for your eventual prosperity, and another boost to the belief that it's really going to happen for you.

SOME ADDITIONAL PROSPERITY BANKING TIPS

You may decide to have several of your accounts in one bank, especially if there aren't a large number of banks conveniently located. It does pay, however, to have your Financial Independence Account in a bank some distance away. This will discourage you from making withdrawals. You can always make your deposits by mail. Leonard Orr tells the story of wanting to go and withdraw the $100 he had in a Financial Independence Account so he could pay half his rent. On the way to the bank at the other end of town, he came up with an idea to earn the money instead. Leonard, in his Money Seminars, also talks about the fact that, if he took that $100 out and paid part of his rent with it, a month later the rent would be due again and he wouldn't have $100 in the bank. So he suggests using your imagination a month earlier to come up with the money some other way. This is part of having a surplus attitude, rather than just making ends meet. If you make a strong effort to produce some money when you're down to your last thousand dollars, rather than down to your last dollar, you'll change your whole financial pattern.

When picking banks, don't worry too

much about how much interest they pay. You won't get rich on interest. Convenience and a pleasant banking environment are much more important criteria.

Don't get so bogged down in such rigid adherence to the concept of seven or eight bank accounts that you don't enjoy the process. You may choose to start one or two accounts and slowly work up to the recommended number. Once you start practicing prosperity consciousness, you will be able to produce substantially more income and may want to have several Financial Independence and Sabbatical accounts. Feel free to mold this concept to your individual needs and desires. The idea is to give yourself a specific direction, and a specific banking program, one that is more functional and more fun than the traditional single bank account.

We often have not learned the simplest truths at an emotional level, where we can apply that knowledge to change our lives for the better. Leonard Orr tells of his three-year struggle to build up a bank account, never seeming to get it going, until he learned a basic truth: The only way you can have less money at the end of the year than at the beginning is by taking it out! Think about that for a while, and about whether you have really learned it at an emotional level. This is the reason for the strict rule against withdrawals from your Financial Independence Account. As long as you never take any money out, that account just has to keep growing. It's simple, commonsense approaches like this that make the difference between poverty and prosperity.

PROSPERITY PROCLAMATIONS

Now is a good time for you once again to experience two Prosperity Proclamations related to banking. By now you may have practiced saying them and writing them. There's a good chance, however, that they have more meaning for you now that you understand the Prosperity Banking concept. It is true, though, that the Prosperity Proclamations can be potent even if, at a conscious level, you are not completely clear as to their meaning. These, however, are among the simplest ones:

EVERY DOLLAR I BANK IS ACCUMULATED WEALTH FOR MY PERSONAL PLEASURE.

I think every bank should print this on every deposit slip and every withdrawal slip, and display it in large letters over every entrance! Obviously, every dollar you bank is building up your wealth. Just as obviously, if you allow yourself to enjoy your money, it is there for your pleasure. The importance of using this truth in a personal proclamation is to convince yourself, at a deep emotional level, that you are indeed accumulating wealth, and that all your money *can* bring you pleasure.

NO MATTER WHAT I DO, MY FINANCIAL WORTH INCREASES EVERY DAY.

This proclamation allows you to focus on the awareness that, as your money earns interest, your financial worth increases. This happens when you are working hard, when you are sleeping, loafing, playing, making love, eating—in fact, whatever you are doing day or night, each and every day. Just accepting this fact can lead to a quantum leap in your prosperity consciousness. One of the main MONEYLOVE concepts is that you are already on the road to prosperity.

Before going on to the next chapter, repeat each of the proclamations out loud twenty times, and write each of them twenty times. As simple as they are, it will take a while for your brain to absorb them completely as a part of your inner knowledge and functional wisdom.

5
Prosperity Investing

The safest way to double your money is to fold it over once and put it in your pocket.
　　—KIN HUBBARD

Goodness is the only investment that never fails.
　　—HENRY DAVID THOREAU

The more prosperity-conscious you become, the better investments you will make. Those who really don't believe in their eventual success will tend to go after fast profits in an investment program that resembles nothing so much as a nervous twitch. Those who have prosperity consciousness approach investing with a calm sense of certainty that more wealth is coming their way.

The MONEYLOVE view of investing is that you can make the most money when you invest for love rather than money, when you invest in an idea rather than in a bunch of figures. For example, a good friend of mine was invited to a backer's audition for a Broadway show. It was *On the Twentieth Century*, written by Betty Comden and Adolph Green, composed by Cy Coleman, directed by Harold Prince, and starring John Cullum, Madeline Kahn, and Imogene Coca. When my friend considered investing $2,000 in the show, because she loved the sampling she saw, many people advised her against investing, citing the statistical truths that most shows, particularly musicals, are flops, and that hardly any ever return the original investment, let alone produce a profit. My friend, however, had just gotten a more prosperous view of her life, which was paying off in increased income, allowed her to think of the $2,000 as surplus money, and allowed her to ignore all the "sensible" advice and become a backer of that show. At this writing, just a few weeks after opening night, it looks like the musical hit of 1978, and my friend could easily triple or quadruple her money. The point is that she believed in the show and invested, not with her mind on how much money she could make, but with a sense of excitement at being a part of something as alive as a Broadway musical. A couple of years ago I attended a backer's audition with some friends, and the producers of the show spent most of the evening talking about how much profit we could all make if we invested. The show wasn't bad, with a clever story and lively music, but that approach turned us off. So far, it hasn't been produced, and I presume any backers lost their entire investments.

REAL ESTATE

Consider those two words: REAL, something that actually exists, genuine, true. ESTATE, a person's property, social standing, ownership of land, degree of prosperity. Those two words are used so often in our culture that we've lost sight of the prosperous sound of them. There is a basic truth that dictates that the prosperity-conscious investor should devote at least a portion of funds to the purchase of real estate: Earth isn't getting any bigger. Earth's population is.

Quite often what determines the difference between someone who owns property and someone who doesn't is their attitude toward owning property. If you've been conditioned to believe that renting an apartment is easier than buying a house or condominium, and gives you more freedom of movement, then you may not even have investigated the fiscal realities. A woman therapist I know was told by her parents that it's always better to own than to rent. At the age of twenty-nine, therefore, with a moderate income, she owned five pieces of property, including two small apartment houses. Another woman I know, earning about $12,000 a year, bought an old house in Richmond, Virginia, fixed it up while she was living in it, and sold it at a healthy profit. She bought another one and found that her credit had soared to the point where she could own two at a time. At last report, she owned eleven houses, with people paying her more than enough rent to pay off the mortgages and provide a healthy profit. Both these women were going against the stereotyped programming that most women receive about owning real estate. At an emotional level, they are told that buying a house is an admission that you never expect to find a man to marry. At a financial level, they are told that buying a house creates more problems than profits. Though, in some isolated instances, both can be true, they usually are not. Each of the women I mention really derived a sense of excitement and pleasure from owning their property, a sense of pride and self-esteem. And this was prosperity consciousness of the highest order!

Check out your own attitudes about real estate. If you focus some of your economic attention on owning instead of renting, you can soon stop renting and start buying.

I personally suggest that Florida and California are the best places to consider investing in real estate, for the simple reason that if everybody in the United States who says he or she wants eventually to move to one of those two states actually does, Florida and California will either have to buy adjoining states to accommodate the crowds or to put gates on their borders. In any event, even if just a portion of those people planning to move West or South to the fastest-growing states do so, the land values have to zoom eventually. And with the colder winters that have recently been experienced in the East and Midwest, and all the scare talk of a new ice age coming, the immigration to the two sun states will accelerate at an even faster pace. One note of warning, however: You must pay attention to basic value when purchasing property in either Florida or California, where land values have greatly increased. I'm certainly not the first person to realize there's a potential huge profit to be made in real estate investments in those two areas.

One tip I'd like to share with you comes from a number of people I know who have made quick and easy profits by buying Florida condominiums. Again, you have to make certain you are not buying at a ridiculously inflated price. The idea is to find a condominium under construction by a reputable corporation, with the completion date at least a year away. Then you put down the minimum down payment. Chances are, the price of the condominium units will go up as completion grows closer, and you can sell out with a substantial profit on your down payment. With the help of a good lawyer, you can arrange to invest in several condominiums at once, and multiply your profits. One friend of mine put down $3,000 on a condominium priced at $32,000. It took a year and a half for the builder to finish the units, and they had soared to $39,000 by that time. She was able to sell her unit, without putting another penny into it, for a neat profit of $7,000, minus commissions, on her $3,000 investment. This may be the best way to invest in condominium property, since I've noticed, in Florida at least, that the biggest jump in price usually occurs between the laying of the foundation and the actual completion date.

Real estate is an investment you should make only with surplus funds, money you can afford to have tied up for a while. It is not as negotiable as stocks, not as accessible as a bank account, and requires a degree of patience and belief not needed for other forms of investment.

One of the myths that keeps people from investing in real estate is that all the good opportunities are long gone. Not true, as there are more real estate opportunities now than ever before, with more possible uses for land, and expanding metropolitan areas, and increased interest in living closer to the land. Some of the negative concepts about real estate are inspired by the experiences of a lot of people's parents. I don't know if you'll identify with this, but many parents talk about "Lost Opportunities in Real Estate," and how they could have bought a piece of land in the 1930s or 1940s that multiplied in value a hundred or a thousand times. Usually this is followed by a statement such as "But of course, who had even $200 to invest in those days?" Who indeed! The truth of the matter is that these wistful reminiscences are usually admissions of acute poverty consciousness. The people involved *could* have come up with $200, if they had really believed in the value of real estate, which they didn't at the time. No one did, which is why it was so cheap. And most of those who bought real estate in those days were more than happy to sell out at the first sign of profit. So few, if any, people made the extraordinary profits indicated by the jump in prices over a long period of time. And the biggest poverty-conscious part of it all is that those real estate investments may be just as sound today, if not more so. Sadly looking back on lost chances can keep you from seeing the real opportunities out there right now! I remember my parents talking in the 1950s about how they could have bought a lot in Wildwood Crest, New Jersey, for about $150 in the late 1940s. When they were talking about it, those lots were selling for several thousand dollars. If, instead of talking, they had bought one of the lots, even at its increased price, I probably would be a millionaire now, instead of having to wait two years. That resort had a boom period, which was inevitable considering its beautiful beaches and the crowding of other Jersey shore resorts. It was just a matter of time, and those same lots were worth hundreds of thousands of dollars! Today, this minute, there are other obvious values in land, places that just have to become more valuable as the increased population looks for new residential and vacation areas. If you have the extra money, and the patience, you can make a fortune in real estate.

STOCKS

The great myth about the stock market is that it involves hard-and-fast financial rules, and logical reactions to economic conditions. Nothing could be further from the truth.

Most people investing in the stock market don't know what the hell they're doing, and this includes a good number of stockbrokers! A lot of people who lose money on the stock market like to accuse brokers of padding their commissions by advising clients to buy and sell at a frenzied pace. I've known a number of brokers, and it's been my experience that they are not so much devious as stupid. Now that I've antagonized an entire industry, let's go on and examine the opportunities in today's stock market.

First off, understand this: Most of the upward and downward swings of stocks have more to do with emotions than any change in the companies' value. Investing your money on this basis would be like betting on whether an overworked executive was going to have a heart attack or nervous breakdown. Putting your money into a stock in the hopes that the majority of people will feel better about the economy a year from now than they do today is just plain dumb. You'd be better off going to the racetrack and picking horses at random.

The best way to invest your money with prosperity consciousness is to put your money into the stock of a company that is constantly and consistently growing, and is doing something you believe in, whether it's manufacturing a product you know and love, or planning exciting projects for the future, or getting into new fields you can personally get enthusiastic about. This will take you beyond mere profit-making as a motive, and give you a personal connection to the stock you buy.

THE LITTLE-OLD-LADY SYSTEM

This is a concept I've borrowed from Leonard Orr and checked out with a number of perceptive and successful stockbrokers. So far, I can't find any flaws in it, and it seems to be about as foolproof a system as any I've yet encountered. It's based on the true fact that little old ladies are the ones with huge investments in the stock market, and huge success. Brokers often despair at the way these little old ladies buy stocks, and it must be frustrating to the brokers to see their profits increase so rapidly. What the little old ladies do that distinguishes them from most other investors is to buy on the basis of the dividend a stock pays. Any broker will tell you that this is not the way to make a profit. I agree that you're not going to earn a fortune from dividends, but that's not the point. What *is* the point is that the ratio of dividend amount to price of stock is an excellent barometer of the basic value of a company. And a system focusing on this obeys the one age-honored rule of the stock market: Buy low and sell high. The way most people do themselves in on buying stocks is by investing all their money when the market is going up, and not being able to buy the many great bargains when it's going down. The LITTLE-OLD-LADY SYSTEM (you can just call it *your* system from now on, if that title bothers you), with some of my own modifications, is as follows:

1. Find a company with at least $100,000,000 in annual sales.
2. Make certain that company has a continuing record of increasing its earnings each year over the past five years.
3. Make certain that company has paid a dividend for the past ten years.
4. Make certain that dividend will give you a higher rate of interest than the bank in which you have your Investment Account.
5. Make certain the company's stock fluctuates enough to give you an opportunity to make a profit.
6. Don't invest more than half of your investment funds initially.

An *ideal* situation would be to find a company that has at least $100,000,000 in sales, with each year's earnings higher than the preceding year for at least the past five years, and paying a regular dividend for the past ten years, a dividend of $.80 on a stock selling for $10, which has been as high as $15 over the past year. There are a number of companies that can provide you with this kind of opportunity. Find a reputable broker to help you. The Standard and Poor's information sheets on each company will provide a lot of this information. Ask your broker to let you see them.

Let's say you have found this ideal situation, and you have $2,000 in your Investment Account. Take $1,000 and buy 100 shares of this company, which we'll call Ideal Opportunity, Inc. The next part of the LITTLE-OLD-LADY SYSTEM is simple:

1. BUY MORE WHEN THE DIVIDEND/PRICE RATIO GOES UP.
2. SELL WHEN THE DIVIDEND/PRICE RATIO GOES DOWN.

This is the one that will have stockbrokers pulling their hair out. But if you really have some prosperity consciousness, you won't allow their opinion to upset or deter you. The system works like this: When the Ideal Opportunity stock rises in price, it will be paying less than 8 percent on stock bought at that increased price, so you sell it. When it falls in price, it will be paying *more* than 8 percent on the decreased price, so buy more. The difference between this and the poverty consciousness way of buying and selling stocks is that most people panic when the price of a stock they've invested in goes down, and they frantically rush to sell it. If it's a sound investment today, it will probably be a sound investment tomorrow, despite the emotional reactions of a large number of stockholders. Their reaction is good for you, for it gives you opportunities to pick up a stock you've decided is a good investment at a much lower price.

Let's go over it again, more specifically this time. You buy the stock at $10. If it goes up to $15, it would now be paying a dividend rate of a little more than 5 percent, instead of the 8 percent at which you bought it. So you sell, taking a neat 50 percent profit! It doesn't matter that you would still be earning 8 percent interest on your original investment. What matters is that the stock is now selling at a rate that pays less than that amount of interest, and this is your signal to sell, to take a profit. You can decide how big a profit you want to take. In fact, I suggest having a clear vision of how much you would be comfortable making on this stock, and selling when it reaches that level.

On the other hand, if the price of Ideal Opportunity, Inc., drops to $8 a share, it would now be paying a dividend of 10 percent to anyone now buying it, so you take some of that unused money in your Investment Account and buy some more, perhaps another 50 shares. If you had tied up all your investment money at the beginning, you wouldn't have been able to take advantage of the drop in price, you wouldn't have been able to buy low. It's an important aspect of your new prosperity consciousness that you see a drop in price as an opportunity to buy more of a good thing rather than a repudiation of your judgment. Some people have so little faith in their own judgment that they consider a drop in the price of a share of stock as some personal failure, losing sight of the normally erratic patterns of stocks.

One underrated and underused tool your broker has to offer you is the *stop-loss*. This is a device whereby you can protect your profits. For example, if your shares of Ideal Opportunity, Inc., which you bought at $10, went up to $14, you could put in a stop-loss at $12. This would mean that, should the stock start down, you would be sold out at $12, or as close to $12 as possible. This would still give you a 20 percent profit. It doesn't pay to keep your stop-loss too close to the current price, since a slight fluctuation could get you out of a stock you want to hold on to for a while. Probably a minimum of 20 percent below the market price would be a good guideline.

USING PROFITS

For your prosperity consciousness, it's necessary to have a specific program for using your profits. This sets your subconscious mind up for the arrival of profits. One way to divide up profits after putting aside enough for taxes is to put:

25 percent in your Investment Account
25 percent in your Financial Independence Account
25 percent in your Pleasure Account
25 percent in your Cash Flow Account

Another way of putting it is to say that a fourth of all you earn through investments is for reinvesting, a fourth to go toward your permanent wealth, a fourth to be spent on personal pleasure, and a fourth to help pay for everyday expenses. This gets you away from the destructive habit of building paper castles in the air. Being wealthy on paper doesn't count when it comes to prosperity consciousness. It's important to get into the habit of *using* your profits, of getting your hands on them, so that they are real for you and can inspire you to even greater profits.

A relative of mine has been investing all his extra money in the stock market for about twenty years. He's made and lost and made again a fortune, *but all on paper!* He's never known the joy of treating himself to a vacation on profits, of having an opulent meal on profits, of paying his rent with profits, or of walking around with his profits in his pocket. He's even almost had a fatal heart attack, worrying about those paper profits!

Many people have unhealthy attitudes about their investments, statements such as:

"I never make money in the stock market."
"With my luck, the company will go bankrupt!"
"I could have been a millionaire if only I'd taken a chance."

Even when said lightheartedly, this kind of statement can be death to your prosperity consciousness. You're too valuable to treat yourself this badly. I can't emphasize too many times that the subconscious mind cannot tell the difference between fact and imagined fact. And this means it can't take a joke! So don't kid about failure, or make self-deprecating statements. These are particularly unhealthy if they are motivated by guilt, by not wanting to admit you are doing very well.

Be an investor rather than a speculator. Don't worry about doubling your money in a month or two. If it doubles in a year or two, you'll be well on your way.

SELF-INVESTING

Another way to invest your money is in yourself. You have many talents, and some of these can be turned into profits if you invest some money in yourself. One way I've done this is to purchase a motor home with my love-partner to travel around and more heavily promote my books. A friend of mine invested $2,000 in a typesetting machine because he wants to publish books on his own. Still another friend had her house extended to accommodate a huge kitchen so she can bake specialty goods and market them to health food stores. Perhaps your way of investing in yourself is to get some specialized education that will enable you to increase your income. You are already your most valuable property, and investing in property improvements is one of the smartest moves you can make in terms of productively using your money!

LEARNING FUND

Whenever I am going to invest in a new area, I set up what I call a LEARNING

FUND. This is money I am willing to risk so that I can learn about this type of investment. I might lose some of it, but that is an investment in my education, not a financial loss. Looking at initial losses this way can help you keep on the path to prosperity. You are not going to be as much of an expert at the beginning as after a few years of investment experience. Learning is a trial and error business, and you may very well have some temporary setbacks. Chalking these up to your Learning Fund will give you a more realistic perspective on what's happening.

A prosperous investor I know does this another way. He calls his initial investments "seed money" and he sees himself planting this money in a new project. If the project doesn't sprout, and he loses some or all of his seed money, he doesn't feel it's a failure, and he considers himself fortunate that he didn't put more substantial amounts of money into the project.

Whatever you invest in, it is easier to deal with the normal ups and downs emotionally if you have a purpose for your profits, and a healthy way of looking at and labeling your losses.

SHORT AND SWEET

I wanted to make this chapter as short and sweet as possible, to take out some of the mystery of investing and some of the complexities that keep people away from using the many investment opportunities in today's economic world. This chapter contains all you need to know to start on a profitable investment program. If you want still more knowledge, fine; there are many good books out on all aspects of investing. But don't use the gathering of more knowledge to delay getting started. You can start your investment program right away by deciding where you want to invest, how much you want to use right now, and what you'd like to do when your profits start coming in.

PROSPERITY PROCLAMATION

The Prosperity Proclamation for this chapter is also simple and to the point:

ALL MY INVESTMENTS ARE PROFITABLE, EITHER IN MONEY OR VALUABLE EXPERIENCE.

Invest some time in writing this one twenty times, and saying it twenty times. Then decide that, if it feels right, you're going to say it to yourself whenever you are considering an investment, or thinking about something you've already invested in.

6
Keeping Afloat
Till Your Ship
Comes In

Money, which represents the prose of life, and which is hardly spoken of in parlors without an apology, is, in its effects and laws, as beautiful as roses.
> —RALPH WALDO EMERSON

It takes as much imagination to create debt as to create income.
> —LEONARD ORR

So far as my coin would stretch; and where it would not, I have used my credit.
> —WILLIAM SHAKESPEARE

How well those live who are comfortably and thoroughly in debt; how they deny themselves nothing; how jolly and easy they are in their minds.
> —THACKERAY

And forgive us our debts, as we forgive our debtors.
> —THE LORD'S PRAYER

Surviving until you become prosperous is not as hard in our current environment as it was in former eras. There are no poorhouses nowadays, no debtors' prisons, and plenty of ways for people with imagination to earn their daily bread, even with a big piece of meat on it. Prosperity consciousness is saying to yourself, "I'll make it, and the money will come," rather than "I wonder how I'm going to make ends meet until things get better." Focusing your energy on what you have rather than what you lack will free your imagination.

A great way to contribute to your self-esteem is to become aware that there are many ways you can earn money. Make a list of ten ways you could earn money right now, if you had to. These are not careers you would necessarily find fulfilling, but just ways to feed yourself until your fortune starts rolling in. One young accountant I know quit his job and decided to meditate on his future and on what he really wanted to do. He didn't have any savings, and in order to explore the kind of work he eventually wanted to do, he got a job as a counterman in a diner, as a temporary office helper, as a waiter, as a scenery mover for a local theater company, and as a cook on a charter sailboat. He held each job, which he considered "research," for only a week or two. He decided that the sailing job was so much fun that he would like to continue this. He borrowed enough money to buy a sailboat and offered gourmet cruises to the Caribbean. His business is now thriving, he is having fun in the sun, and he is meeting a lot of wealthy people to inspire his own prosperity consciousness. He always knows he can earn a living even if this business doesn't work out. Do you know this for yourself? Look in the want ads of your local paper. As your prosperity consciousness emerges, you might consider selling for some company. There are always lots of sales jobs, and with some self-confidence that you can project, you can always earn a healthy amount of money selling.

But understand that you don't have to even go this far. We live in an almost failure-proof society. I've said it several times, and it's worth repeating: In this society you really have to be very stupid and work very hard to fail.

USING MONEY THAT ISN'T YOURS

For some six years, I survived using other people's money. I consider this an investment on their part, a bond of trust between us. I believed in my eventual prosperity, and I assume some of the banks I dealt with had this same faith. A struggling writer is not the best credit risk, but there are ways to get around even this, and I will share some of them with you. But before I do that, it's important that you develop a healthy respect for credit, and for yourself as a borrower. If you feel borrowing money is sinful, or a sign of failure, consider the wealthiest people in our nation. Few of them are debt-free. Many of them owe millions of dollars. In fact, until you can borrow a million dollars, in our economic structure, you will not be considered as having arrived. People's owing money is what keeps our economy going. The banks earn interest on those debts, and they pay this interest to their depositors, and the depositors spend that interest on consumer goods. It's just another way of circulating money.

Of course, the trick is to borrow money when you don't need it. When I was gainfully employed in broadcasting, I borrowed $600 from a bank. I didn't need it at all, and I paid back the one-year loan in two months. This gave me an excellent credit rating, and the bank offered me a $5,000 credit line, on my signature alone. I lived off that credit line for a long time. As long as I kept up the monthly payments, my credit was good with that bank, even in periods when I earned little or no money. Some things you need to know about credit:

1. When you borrow money, a creditor considers you an asset.

This surprises many people, but is a book-keeping fact. As a debtor, you become an account receivable, and the creditor can borrow money against the money you owe, and consider that money as tangible assets.

2. Credit departments can be reasonable and help you solve your problems.

This surprises even more people, many of whom consider credit departments as the enemy. Not true—they're as anxious as you for you to get your financial act together.

3. Creditors like to hear from you, and get worried when they don't.

In order for you to continue to be considered an asset, the creditors have to have some indication that you will eventually pay up. If you give them the silent treatment, they can panic and start sending threatening letters and making intimidating phone calls. It pays for you to let them know you are planning to make a lot of money and will definitely pay them as soon as possible. If you can send some small amount as a sign of good faith, so much the better, but a letter will often hold them off and keep them satisfied for months.

4. Nasty letters and phone calls are signs of impotence on the part of creditors.

As in most such instances, if they really

had much power, they wouldn't have to get hostile. Most dunning letters and threatening phone calls have no legal force behind them, though a lot of companies try to create the illusion they do, and many even have subsidiary "law" or "collection" firms that give you the impression they have passed on your debt to a more authoritarian organization. One such creditor told a friend of mine, "We wish you would either declare bankruptcy, tell us when you'll pay, or tell us you'll never pay, just so we can write you off the books."

5. If you don't have income or assets, there is nothing anyone can do about the money you owe them.

If creditors go to court, which they try to avoid under all but the most desperate circumstances, the most they can get is a judgment against you, which will attach some of your "future earnings." In other words, the basic rule still applies: They can't get it until you get it. I find that if you sincerely tell creditors that you don't have the cash now, and will pay your bill as soon as you do have it, they'll leave you alone.

6. Anyone who loans you money is exhibiting faith in your eventual prosperity.

Creditors want to believe you are going to succeed and be able to easily pay them back. They realize they have little legal recourse if you don't, so they really are trusting you to keep your word.

7. You may be doing your creditors a favor by delaying payment.

For a long while, as I struggled toward prosperity, I used to take every chunk of money I received and immediately use it up paying bills. As I began to understand more about money, I realized this was foolish. Paying bills so that I was broke again kept me focusing my attention on survival instead of surplus, and made my payments few and far between. As soon as I started changing this habit, and only paying a little bit when I got a large amount of money and using that money instead to creatively produce more money, I got out of the vicious cycle, and was able to pay back my creditors at a much more rapid pace.

8. Borrowed money is income until you have to pay it back.

Part of the poverty consciousness "work ethic" is to consider owing money as a horrible bad habit, and a burden that must be lifted as soon as possible. But the money someone loans you *is* an act of faith, and even a gamble on the part of the lender. This is the awareness you should focus on if you want to create the right emotional climate for paying the loan back as fast as possible, and as easily as possible. It certainly behooves you to have at least as much faith in your own pending prosperity as does your creditor. One way to do this is to consider that money as an asset, just as the creditor considers you as one, and not as a liability. When you pay it back it is a current expense, not something you've been allowing to hang over your head creating anxiety and discomfort for months or years.

9. Because of inflation, you usually come out ahead by borrowing money.

Wealthy people have always known this and delay paying back borrowed money as long as possible. If you borrowed a large sum of money ten years ago, even considering interest payments, the money you pay off that loan with today will be worth a lot less. Meanwhile, you've had use of it all that time. If you used it creatively, it should have enhanced your earning power in some way. If your earnings have increased at a normal rate along with the inflationary cycle, it would take you fewer hours today to earn the money than it did ten years ago. You could really look at it as borrowing time. If you have to work a month right now to earn $1,000, and borrow $1,000, and get prosperous enough so you can earn $1,000 in a day or week, you'll be well ahead of the game when you pay the loan back.

10. The more you convince yourself of your eventual prosperity, the easier it will be to convince creditors, and the happier they'll be to keep you on the books.

It sometimes seems as if creditors actually love having wealthy people delay payment. They certainly bend over backwards to extend every courtesy, and hardly ever resort to the nasty approach. Your creditors *want* to believe you can easily pay them back. They love giving you the benefit of the doubt if you can give them the slightest indication that your financial status is on the upswing. They offer you lots of opportunities to practice your prosperity consciousness, and to use your creative imagination. And in the final analysis, they cannot argue with the basic existential statement: "When I get it, you'll get it!" Some people beat themselves over the head with their debts, rather than having the attitude toward creditors of gratitude for allowing them to survive a bit longer, and buying them the freedom to become more prosperous. A good attitude to have toward all creditors, regardless of the amount owed, is: I WILL EASILY PAY YOU WITH A PORTION OF MY FORTHCOMING SURPLUS.

Being in debt can help you produce more money. When I sold one of my first books to a major publisher, I told that firm that I needed enough money up front to pay off my debts for six months. I got it, and then wrote the book in a month, thereby having five free months in which to relax and not have to consider myself as someone in debt. I also used some of that money to help promote the book, thereby increasing my income. By telling the publisher I needed to have my debts cleared up for six months to free my mind to write, I also realized the value of having a free mind—and realized as well that I could have freed mine even if they hadn't given me the money, merely by changing my attitude about the money I owed!

I suppose the basic message here is to feel okay about yourself if you borrow money, to consider your creditors as your helpers on the road to prosperity, and not to let the fact you owe money get in the way of prosperous feelings about yourself. One note, though: Don't get in the trap of borrowing money just to hold off financial crisis. If you need $200 to pay this month's rent, you would be much better off using your creative imagination to produce that $200. The rent will be due again in another month, so you may as well produce the additional income now as then. If possible, borrow money only when you want it for some purpose that will eventually produce more income. As you begin to think more prosperous thoughts, you'll be able to use borrowed money to make tremendous profits. Borrowing for investments is a sound practice, as long as you invest rather than speculate. Borrowing money to put it into your Financial Independence Account also makes a lot of sense, since just having it there will produce a feeling of prosperity worth far more than the difference in the interest you pay out over and beyond the interest you earn.

Don't participate in the negative programming game of feeling guilty about your debts. This is stuff others taught you. Just consider yourself as prosperous as the many solvent businesses that are heavily in debt, and the many wealthy people, and the biggest debtor of them all: the United States government, which goes so far as to borrow money it *knows* it can never pay back. This can be good for you, however, because it helps produce the inflationary cycle that you can take advantage of to earn greater amounts of money. Borrowing money can be a good investment. Again, the money you pay back in the future should cost you less in terms of earning hours than when you borrowed it. If you are learning anything at all from this book, it should cost you a lot less of your time energy in the future to produce the same amount of money. So if you earn $12,000 a year now, and borrow $1,000, it will pay you to wait until your income goes up to $120,000 a year, so that it will cost you only a tenth of the time to pay back that loan amount.

Stay away from companies that offer to consolidate your loans. All they are doing is charging you a hefty fee to do what you could easily do for yourself. They'll add up all your debts, figure out how much you can afford to pay out based on your current income, and then write letters to your creditors saying you can only pay back the loan at such and such a rate. Your creditors will be just as willing to take less per month if you write them yourself, and you'll save the fee.

Worrying about debts is one of the most nonproductive and poverty-conscious things you can do. I never worry about debts. When I was heavily in debt, I would have preferred not being in debt, but I realized that I wasn't going to get out from under unless I put my mind to work *instead of* to worry.

Here's a useful technique in dealing with debt worries. Plan to focus your attention on the money you owe once each month. Look over your bills, pay the ones you can, express any pain, anger, or frustration you have about not being able to pay them all, and put the rest in a drawer and forget about them. Even if you have to jump up and down and scream to purge yourself of worry over debt, do so. Then don't think about it for the rest of the month. Understand that the bills in that drawer are fantasy once they're out of sight, while the money in your pocket is reality. In conjunction with this technique, you can write each individual concern over money on a separate piece of paper, and stuff it all in that drawer with the unpaid bills.

Remember, the best thing you can do for your creditors is stay healthy and substantially increase your earning power. They are already earning money off your indebtedness, and are more than willing to continue doing so as long as they can justify their faith in you. The thousands of banks, savings and loan associations, and credit companies who are frantically trying to loan out their money are not doing it out of the goodness of their hearts. They make money loaning it out, just as you can make money borrowing it. This is Prosperity Circulation in action. There are all sorts of positive aspects to owing money, and where you focus your attention is what you get in terms of consciousness. You owe it to yourself to focus on prosperity, and that's the only debt or obligation you should be putting energy into right now.

GETTING STARTED

Remember that first admonition by William James for effecting personal change: Start immediately. No matter what your current financial status, you can start using the techniques and skills in this book. The less you start with, the more spectacular your accomplishments will be. When I do MONEYLOVE seminars, the audience is usually divided between wealthy people and people of little or no income, including a number of artists and writers. I always find it fascinating that the lower-income members of the audience seem to identify more easily with prosperity consciousness. The wealthy, usually there because they are not enjoying their money, get excited about the ideas, but it's a subdued excitement, born out of cynicism and self-doubt. Often the wealthy participants in my seminars even display an aura of desperation, as if to say, "I've worked hard, and accumulated a lot of money, and it hasn't been worth it. Please show me a way to get more out of life." One couple of obvious wealth came up to me at the end of a seminar, and the woman said, "My husband made a half-million dollars this past year, but he still acts like he did when he was making fifteen thousand. I've tried threatening him, telling him that if he didn't loosen up and start enjoying our money, I was going to leave him and take him for every cent I could get. But I love him, and I want us both to enjoy that money." There were tears in her eyes. The husband's eyes were also moist. I agreed to work with him privately. Part of that work involved giving him specific fun things to do with his money. It was probably the hardest work he had ever done, using his money for pleasure. And it took several months to get him to a place where he could continue on his own. I think this illustrates that lots of money is sometimes an obstacle to prosperity consciousness. If you are used to very little money, you can get much more excited about the prospect of more prosperity. Just as sunshine would not be so sweet if it weren't for the night, prosperity wouldn't feel so good if it weren't for the fact that most of us are not born into wealth. But it's the feeling good that's important, and you can start that right now, without earning another penny.

Every time you are broke, you are getting a priceless opportunity to use your creative imagination and prove how prosperous you really are. Never lose sight of the fact that you are a valuable, income-producing property, worth investing lots of time and money in. All it takes is one push of the starter button to get going. And the most exciting news of all is that *you* get to push your own button!

PUSHING YOUR OWN BUTTON

We represent the highest form of life on earth and, so far as we know, the highest form in the universe. And yet we are far from perfect. We have inherited an abundant planet, and have created poverty as a physical manifestation of emotional fears. This book is aimed at providing you with resources in the form of new ideas, techniques, and habits. These resources can return you to your natural state of prosperity. This book is just a seed. You must make a decision to plant it in your subconscious, and nourish it with positive action.

Getting started immediately means starting to appreciate the prosperous things in your life right now. You are already rich in terms of time. You couldn't buy an extra healthy day of life for a million dollars. A prominent stockbroker told me he can always tell the difference between potential customers of wealth and those of more modest means. He says the wealthy always say what they have to say in the shortest possible amount of time, obviously considering their time valuable. *Your* time is valuable, and you can add to that value by more effectively using that time. Some ways to do this:

1. Whenever you make a commitment of time, ask youself, "How is this effort moving me closer to prosperity?"
2. Whenever you communicate with someone, get to the heart of the matter.
3. Realize that scientists have used billions of dollars *just* to extend your life and buy you extra time.
4. Understand that a moment unpleasantly spent can destroy the benefits of weeks of positive action.
5. Make your decisions as quickly as possible.

QUICK DECISIONS

A lot of people have difficulty with the last item on the preceding list, making decisions quickly. This may be one of the greatest differences between someone who is bogged down in poverty consciousness and the prosperous thinker. Often it doesn't matter what decision you make, as long as you make it quickly. I have made decisions that turned out to be wrong, and went back and did it another way, and still took less time than many who procrastinated over the original decision! You are exercising your brain's lightning-quick power when you make a quick decision, and this is more important than the temporary results of the decision itself. Your brain is capable of handling 140,000 million bits of information in one second, and if you take hours or days or weeks to reach a vital decision, you are short-circuiting your most valuable property! And saying to yourself "I can't decide" is exactly what creates your inability to decide.

Having a sense of momentum in your life will help you use time more effectively. And you'll be able to create more usable time as you get more involved and excited about your life. It's a well-known fact that people who are pursuing some task or activity that excites and interests them need less sleep. If you are now getting eight hours a night, think what you could do with two more hours a day, fourteen more a week.

Though it's good to have as many alternatives in your life as possible, sometimes these can use up too much time and dilute your energy. Particularly if you have to focus a lot of attention on choosing among them. I've used the analogy of a trapeze artist not being willing to let go of the old trapeze bar before grabbing the new one, but other people sabotage themselves by filling their lives with a lot of new trapeze bars, to give themselves a greater sense of safety. This can just as easily add to confusion as to safety. If you take that extra moment to decide which bar to grab, it could be your last moment. It probably pays, at the beginning of building your prosperity consciousness, to have that clear vision focused on one specific destination. The healthiest and most productive behavior seems to be to have an awareness of your alternatives but to pay attention to, and focus your energy on, just one at a time.

VIEW OF THE WORLD

The way you see the world is a direct reflection of your self-esteem. If you see the world as filled with hungry people, you'll never be able to throw off the bonds of poverty consciousness. True, there are people starving in the world today, but to say that this is a permanent condition, or that it's going to get worse, is taking a very narrow view of the situation. The human brain has always managed to come up with solutions before, and enough people of creative imagination are now working toward that end to guarantee an end to hunger in our lifetime. There are enough resources on the planet right now to richly feed every man, woman, and child. Limited initiative and limited imagination have prevented the harnessing of those resources, but this is rapidly changing. Do what you can to help humanity, but understand that the best thing you can do is to harness your own resources, and make the most of your own potential, so that you will have an even greater effect when you do for others.

If your view of the world includes a feeling that all the great ideas and inventions have already been created, think again. This was also the commonly held belief a thousand years ago, and a hundred years ago. In 1900 people thought such inventions as the light bulb, telephone, and automobile had taken humankind to the outer limits of inventive accomplishment. They were wrong, and those who say the same thing today are just as wrong! There has never been more opportunity for the man or woman with clear vision, belief, and practical skills.

Give yourself a healthy and prosperous new view of the world. Each day, experience as many of its wonders as possible. This is still an abundant planet. Find the evidence of this yourself. Explore the towers of commerce; walk into a stock brokerage house and see the signs of economic strength and vitality; take a trip to the country and enjoy the splendors of nature; and pay attention to all the truly alive people who populate your world, and begin to see that this world of yours is *really* yours to view and do with as you will!

Each time you encounter someone, you might silently say, "I am wonderful, and so are you!"

Poverty *is* a manmade disease, and not based on any natural laws.

PROSPERITY CURIOSITY

Curiosity is often cited as a vital factor in achieving wealth. I agree, but there are different types of curiosity. Some types of curiosity bog you down in endless detail. You don't have to know the secret of life to enjoy it. You don't have to know how a radio works if you can hear the music. You don't have to know which ninety muscles your brain activates for every breath you take in order to savor that breath. And you don't have to know the intimate details of the workings of your brain in order to tap into its tremendous power. You can, however, be curious in a prosperity-conscious way. Some useful questions to ask yourself:

1. How can I be more creative in my everyday life?
2. What can I learn from my daily environment?
3. How can I apply some of the world's great ideas to my own life?
4. How can I reach out to people in new ways?
5. How can I make this day different from every other day?

Looking at temporary setbacks with a sense of curiosity rather than despair also increases your prosperity consciousness. Ask:

1. What can I learn from the way this turned out?
2. How could I have done it better?
3. What should I keep and what should I discard from this experience?
4. How can I use this result to further my prosperity plans?

Multimillionaire Charles Schwab once said, "I have failed 49 percent of the time and succeeded only 51 percent of the time." But that success rate was more than enough to bring him all he desired. A baseball star can achieve heroic stature with a batting average of .400, meaning he missed the ball six out of ten times! So stop putting yourself down for being human, for experiencing what every successful human being has always experienced: temporary setbacks that provide you with valuable learning material.

You now know all you need to know to achieve all the success in life you could possibly desire. Wisdom, however, is not knowledge. Wisdom is the application of knowledge. The question to ask yourself, then, and maybe the best example of prosperity curiosity there could be, is *"What do I now know that I can apply more effectively and successfully?"*

YOU'VE ALREADY STARTED

The process of becoming prosperous has already begun for you. Just absorbing the information in this book at a conscious level has effected some changes at a subconscious level. There have been thoughts and concepts constantly repeated throughout these six chapters. The cells of your brain most intensely record those thoughts and ideas that are most often repeated. This is the way you can most successfully start pushing your own button. Giving yourself new prosperity attitudes and habits will prepare you emotionally for the money that is certain to come your way. The seeds you plant through positive action and positive imagination will grow quickly and firmly. Watch the words you use, as they, too, take root. I remember as a child my mother saying, "You talk so much, you'll become either a lawyer or a radio announcer." When I got to NBC, I reminded my mother that those words were probably directly responsible!

Still another prosperity technique you might use to focus more sharply on the positive use of words is to buy a dictionary, or use one you already have, and cross out every single negative word. *Fail. Poor. Suffer.* Cross them all out. Maybe you can take a few minutes each night to work on this project. Don't rush. Really allow the emotional impact of what you are doing to fill your being.

SOME SELF-STARTERS

MONEYLOVE is filled with strategies and techniques and ideas, any of which can help you get started. And each of these can suggest new ones to you. Here are a few more.

1. Have a specific daily goal each day. This can be to come up with a new idea, to learn a new word, to use your money in a new way, to meet someone who can offer you advice or support. Thinking in terms of the number 10 can be a good stimulus. You might set daily goals to:

a. Put $10 aside.
b. Write 10 pages in a personal journal.

c. Spend 10 minutes in silent reflection.
d. Call an old friend and spend 10 minutes talking over old times.
e. Think of 10 positive things you can do in the next week.
f. Come up with 10 things that make you feel good and lift your spirits.

This last one is a great way to combat temporary setbacks. If you always have ten ways to defeat gloom, you'll never use up too much time in self-pity. One way I prepare for those times when things don't go just the way I want them is always to have at least ten mystery novels I haven't read. I can lose myself in a good mystery no matter what is happening in my life. I find that by deeply involving my conscious mind in *whodunit*, my subconscious mind often comes up with a way *I can do it better*.

2. Become familiar with money. Have you ever really studied a dollar bill? It's a veritable gallery of fine art and religious and mystical symbolism.

3. Become an expert in some area that now interests you. Learn as much as you can about it. This will build your confidence and serve you well even if you never get to use all the knowledge. But it *must* be a subject you enjoy.

4. Start to act prosperous. Ask yourself, "Would I say this? Would I do this? Would I feel this way, if I were rich?" People most often judge your degree of wealth by the phys-

ical attitude you present. If you walk, talk, and dress like a million dollars, the people you meet and deal with will assume you already have it. For several hundred dollars, you can look the part.

5. Daydream. You'll never achieve your fondest dreams if you don't give yourself conscious time to have those dreams. Play with some of the fantasies in this book, invent some of your own. Another MONEYLOVE FANTASY to try on for size: Imagine you knew for certain that you were going to receive a million dollars in exactly one year. How would this affect what you are now doing? How would you most like to use the next twelve months preparing for your windfall? You won't have the money, so the next year will change mainly because of a change in your attitude. And *that* is what prosperity consciousness is all about!

6. Practice thinking big. Write a check for a million dollars. One man I knew wrote just such a check and presented it to his wife for her birthday. He told her, "The pleasure I got from imagining what it would be like to actually write you a check for a million dollars is all I need to know for sure I'll make it someday."

7. Realize you are the creator of your own personality, not other people. Again, poverty comes from outside, prosperity from within. We all have the capacity to become whomever we choose. This was never brought home to me more clearly than as a shy nineteen-

year-old radio announcer in a new town. I decided to project another part of my personality rather than the bookish bespectacled one I had projected at home. I got contact lenses and some sharp clothes, and started feeling more attractive and more sure of myself. I found out something amazing. In a new town, with new people, there was no preconception of me. They had no memory of me as a shy kid with glasses, and so they were willing to accept the image I sent out. Maybe you can give yourself some similar experiences. Take a trip to a strange town, and pretend that you have suddenly eliminated all your doubt and fear, and allowed all your positive traits to come forward. This isn't being phony, since you are merely expressing some of the unexpressed parts of you. Shut down your own memories of the negative, poverty-conscious parts of you, and allow this new person to take hold. When you return to your own environment, don't be surprised if your friends and loved ones don't notice the difference right away. They are still focused on the you that was, and it will take a while for them to recognize the change. You won't have to beat them over the head with it. As you get used to yourself as prosperous, confident, and imaginative, others will begin to be impressed with these qualities. It took quite a while for my friends back home to see the changes in me. That wasn't important, for I had made a new life for myself in my new town and with my new strength. Others can only drag you down if you give them that power.

One way to give others power over you is to tell them everything you are doing to become prosperous before they are ready to hear it. Not everyone can accept the idea of prosperity consciousness, and you are not doing yourself a favor by trying to convince them. They'll be convinced soon enough when the results start coming in, when it will be too late for their negative comments to have any effect, and too late for their poverty consciousness to interrupt your flow and energy.

Finally, realize that the truly prosperous individual is a giver, so practice this aspect of your new life-style as well. Be willing to listen to others, to offer help, and to share prosperous ideas. If you are selling goods or services, always give people more than their money's worth, and you will prosper even more rapidly. Don't sacrifice your own growth, don't waste your valuable time with people who aren't ready to receive what you have to offer, and don't try to change other people or the world. You can change only yourself, and that's a lifetime job!

Also remember that it isn't money that brings the real satisfaction to a prosperous person. It's the sense of doing something important, making a valuable contribution. Without this, money means nothing. With it, you own the world!